D1420442

LINGUISTICS AS A SCIENCE

Linguistics as a Science

VICTOR H. YNGVE

INDIANA UNIVERSITY PRESS
Bloomington & Indianapolis

Manufactured in the United States of America

Library of Congress Cataloging-in-Publication Data
Yngve, Victor H., 1920–
  Linguistics as a science

  Bibliography: p.
  Includes index.
  1. Linguistics.   I. Title.
P121.Y55   1986   410   85-45579
ISBN 0-253-33439-X

1 2 3 4 5 90 89 88 87 86

CONTENTS

PREFACE

Can linguistics achieve its long-standing goal of becoming a science, or must it turn back to philosophy and renew its dependence on logic and the theory of knowledge?

Linguistics seems poised today at the point where physics was several centuries ago. Ancient preconceptions still block its way to modern science, not having been pushed very far aside by the newer methods. This essay attempts to remove some of the obstacles left in the path by tradition, and press on in the direction of science.

The history of science clearly shows that any idea, assumption, or theory—no matter how arrived at, no matter how new or how encrusted with tradition—must pass the tests of comparison against observational evidence before it can be allowed to survive as a part of science. There is no shortcut or substitute for the program and methods of science. Our only defense against fictions, fads, and false prophets is to refuse to believe anything that has not been scientifically justified, no matter how intuitive, rational, or modish it may seem.

When theories have been tested and shown to agree with observation, we may accept them tentatively, pending further tests against additional evidence should any doubts arise. Even the testing of theories that prove to be false sometimes has the positive effect of pointing the way to newer theories that better accord with the evidence. Observation and experiment also sometimes reveal unforeseen phenomena and thus lead to new discoveries. By these means science has saved us from error and has increased our secure understanding of nature.

We attempt here a consistent application of the program and methods of modern science to the problems of linguistics. Some of the most strongly held traditional views in the discipline are tested. They do not agree with the evidence and must be rejected. Out of this grows a new position that passes the same preliminary tests. Then the two positions are put to further test against a wider range of observational evidence.

I wish to acknowledge the great debt of gratitude that I owe to my teachers in the University of Chicago Department of Physics around 1950, particularly my dissertation advisor, Marcel Schein, and many stimulating professors, among them Samuel K. Allison, Enrico Fermi, Murray Gell-Mann, Frank C. Hoyt, Ernest H. Hutten, Maria Goeppert Mayer, John R. Platt, Edward Teller, Harold Voorhees, Gregor Wentzel, William H. Zachariasen, and Clarence Zener. I have tried to follow the vision of science that they imparted.

An early version of some of the material presented here on the two alternatives facing linguistics was read to the linguistics departments of the University of Chicago and of Northwestern University in March 1981, and distributed informally. In August 1982 a short paper was presented to the Linguistic Association of Canada and the United States (LACUS) and subsequently published in the proceedings, followed in the next three years by three more papers there. The discussions resulting from these presentations, and other informal discussions with students and colleagues over the years, have helped me to foresee and try to meet many of the usual sorts of objections. I have been particularly aided in coming to terms with the subject by comments, sometimes unwitting, sometimes pointed, sometimes studied, from Jan Terje Faarlund, Donald W. Fiske, Kenneth E. Foote, Robert A. Fox, Paul Friedrich, Eric P. Hamp, Charles F. Hockett, Carol L. Hofbauer, Ilene Lanin-Kettering, James D. McCawley,

Eugene A. Nida, W. Keith Percival, Barbara Rubenstein, Michael Silverstein, Don R. Swanson, Stuart-Morgan Vance, and Margaret Zabor.

Preliminary versions of the manuscript were read by Daniel G. Freedman, John Goldsmith, Sol H. Krasner, Karen Landahl, Leonard Linsky, Johanna Nichols, Milton B. Singer, and Dorin Uritescu. I have appreciated their reactions and hope they will approve of the final form.

I should particularly like to thank Arnold C. Satterthwait for reading the manuscript with care at a crucial juncture and providing valuable criticisms and suggestions.

Finally, I wish to acknowledge the importance to this research of the environment afforded by the University of Chicago, which encourages and facilitates interdisciplinary research. I have particularly appreciated the spirit of academic tolerance and friendliness cultivated by its Department of Linguistics, and the quality and depth of the collection housed in its Library. The University has provided research funds from the Spencer Foundation and the Benton Education Research Fund, and from the Division of the Social Sciences, The Division of the Humanities, and the Graduate Library School.

I have also enjoyed the considerable benefits of membership in the Linguistic Association of Canada and the United States (LACUS). Its campaign against narrow-mindedness, sectarianism, and dogma in linguistics and related disciplines makes a major contribution to linguistic life, and the quality of the colleagueship that it offers is outstanding.

To my wife, Jean H. Yngve, who has helped more than she can know, I give my heartfelt thanks, and to her I dedicate this book.

Victor H. Yngve

Dune Acres, Indiana
May, 1986

CHAPTER ONE

Questions and Clues

It has been more than a century and a half since the founding of modern scientific linguistics, yet serious questions have arisen regarding the intellectual health of the discipline and its status as a science. The history of linguistics shows a succession of theoretical positions, each welcomed with hope but later abandoned in favor of the next. Today there is a growing suspicion that the leading theoretical thrust of the last fifteen or twenty years is also inadequate, and that none of the many other existing types of grammar offers an acceptable alternative.

Linguists working in what has been called the mainstream have become increasingly aware of serious theoretical difficulties in the foundations of linguistics. There is an undercurrent of uneasiness, a feeling that we may have lost our bearings. The leading body of theory has been subjected to intensive criticism, and serious disagreements have sprung up even among its defenders, impeding their efforts to establish an adequate theoretical framework. Attempts to repair perceived shortcomings have given rise to new versions of linguistic theory. These take their place among the ever-widening group of divergent points of view, and thus tend to feed the fires of controversy rather than settle the issues that stimulated their development. The resulting multiplicity of theories has been called a post-revolutionary chaos (Binnick 1981).[1]

Perhaps this diversity should not be seen as disturbing. Perhaps one should argue that a choice of linguistic theory is a matter of utility, taste, opinion, or fashion like a preference for one style of clothing over another, or that it is more like religious belief or political persuasion, where people may honestly differ in their views but each covets the right to hold firm to his own credo, and in a pluralistic society freely grants to others the right to be wrong.

But this book sees linguistics rather as a scientific enterprise devoted to understanding a complex and fascinating aspect of nature: the way in which humans communicate with each other. In its search for understanding, science tries to settle controversies rather than simply tolerate them. It does this by seeking publicly available and reproducible evidence that bears on the truth or falsity of disputed points of theory, and by seeking theoretical positions that are subject to test against publicly available and reproducible evidence. In this way science tries to eliminate false conceptions and increase our secure understanding of nature. From this point of view the current trend is indeed disturbing.

With the increasing proliferation of approaches, an adequate agreed-upon body of explicit formal theory seems far beyond our grasp. One cannot have a science when no two major theoreticians can agree on the proper shape of theory. The purpose of theory is to unify the observations in a field and make them understandable by interrelating them to one another and providing insight, but this is difficult or impossible if different investigators use different theories. We are left in confusion as to where the truth might lie.

There are complaints that the leading theories do not properly address large areas of data (Weinreich, Labov, and Herzog 1968; Hymes 1974; Dingwall 1971; Derwing 1973; Gross 1979; Naro 1980; and many others). Linguists dealing with observational data face the problem that no matter which formal grammatical framework they might consider for guiding their research and presenting their results, it will be unacceptable to a part of the potential readership. Then in the end it may turn out to be inadequate for the purpose, and there is always the risk that before the fieldwork has been completed the chosen position may already have become obsolete in the eyes of its own designers. For these reasons, observational or data-oriented work is often put forward with a bare minimum of formal theory. As a result the research suffers, and with it the discipline, for observations unconnected to adequate integrating and interrelating theory are little more than a mass of unorganized facts, and thus only a feeble contribution to linguistic knowledge.

Theoretical work finds itself equally handicapped. Insights captured within one grammatical framework may be difficult or impossible to state in other frameworks which accommodate other sets of insights. When frameworks change, the insights that they have fostered may become orphaned and in danger of being lost through lack of support, or abandoned and forgotten altogether. Indeed, many valuable results of earlier eras have already met this fate.

A perceived need for theory able to confront a broader range of communicative concerns has propelled renewed exploration in the area of semiotics. But authors lament the incompatibility between semiotic theory and grammatical theory. Work in the area of pragmatics also faces difficulties in integrating its results into the rest of linguistic theory, and the same is true for work in semantics.

Perhaps the diversity of theory should be seen instead as a healthy sign— the greater the diversity, the greater the chance of someone finding a satisfactory solution. Or there may be a hope that the best from many approaches can someday be incorporated in a grand synthesis. But a quarter century has gone by since the beginning of transformational-generative grammar, which was once a great hope, and there is no sign yet of significant convergence. Instead, the diversity and eclecticism of theory are actually increasing. Every new form of grammar that is launched testifies to perceived inadequacies in earlier forms and raises the suspicion that not one of our theories is really adequate. With an abundance of inadequate theories, it is not at all clear where next to turn.

If our theories are not adequate, our results are suspect. This could have widespread consequences beyond the boundaries of linguistics itself. Consider the importance of human speech and communication in establishing and maintaining social groups, and in carrying much of our culture. Consider that linguistic concepts and results are frequently borrowed by other disciplines, such as psycholinguistics, cognitive psychology, anthropology, social psychology, sociology, human development, and studies of aphasia and communicative disorders. Consider also the importance of speech, writing, and communication in the humanities. It would seem that any question concerning the intellectual and scientific integrity of linguistics would raise issues of considerable urgency.

If one compares linguistics to physics, the contrasts between the two sciences are striking. In place of the instability of linguistic theory, physics has a large body of standard theory and results on which a large curriculum can be based that is not much different from one university to another. Unlike the situation in linguistics, where major linguists seldom agree on theory, major physicists around the world generally agree about most matters of theory.

True, there are sharp differences of opinion in certain unsettled frontier areas of research, such as the identity and structure of the elementary particles and the nature of the associated forces. However, these differences of opinion find expression in explicit hypotheses and theories, and there is frenzied activity by experimentalists to find objective evidence for testing some of the predictions of the theories so as to be able to decide among them or obtain hints leading to other more satisfactory theories.

One finds the testing of predictions in linguistics, too, but mainly the details of theory within one or another of the leading paradigms. Major differences between different paradigms are seldom the occasion for massive searches for observational evidence to be used in deciding among them. Instead, other less-conclusive arguments are brought forward.

These differences between the conduct of research in linguistics and in physics may well provide important clues to what might underlie the widely admitted problems in linguistics. If theory is unstable, if competing theories abound, if there is difficulty in choosing among different theories, there may be problems related to the criteria of truth that are used in the discipline, the methods that are employed to determine what to accept tentatively and what to reject as false or probably false. Thus it may be that we are not just having difficulties discovering the correct form of grammar. Perhaps the problems are at a more basic level common to all the approaches.

Since that is a possibility, it seems appropriate and worthwhile to step back and reexamine the foundations and basic assumptions of linguistics. If we find the foundations to be in good order, we may be reassured at least on that point, and can then move on and look elsewhere. But if they are not in good order, we might still be ahead, for our examination may already have uncovered the source of the difficulties. Perhaps then it would be clear how to repair the foundations, or how to lay new ones on which to build a stronger discipline.

CHAPTER TWO

Language and Linguistics

Before starting to examine the foundations of linguistics, we need to lay out in plain view a few items of general agreement that are not often stated explicitly. These include a brief inventory of the current scope and dimensions of the discipline and some important points concerning language and science. These will probably be known and understood by most readers, but since they will be assumed as common background, a brief review may not be out of place.

LINGUISTICS

It is clear that the term *linguistics* does not in itself define or delimit our area of study for us, least of all from its etymology. It does not carry any theoretical presuppositions that we are more concerned with the tongue than with the lips, the larynx, or the ears, or that we would necessarily rule out the study of gestural systems used by the deaf or by Australian aboriginal tribes. It is simply the conventional name in English for a discipline that would be the same by any other name.

The discipline of linguistics is understood instead in terms of a certain group of professionals, a cohesive literature, professional societies and meetings, organized faculties and graduate programs, and a set of interests and questions in relation to a currently agreed-upon range of observational phenomena. It reflects the existing division of labor in science.

Linguistics is not necessarily tied to a particular methodology or type of theory, for these are seen as means to the end of understanding the various phenomena that present themselves. Thus the named discipline is more subject to change than the name as new phenomena are explored, new methods utilized, new theories proposed, and new knowledge gained. Linguistics today is certainly much different from what it was when the name was first applied over a hundred years ago, and from what it was as recently as 1950, or even 1965.

The scope of data of interest to linguists includes ancient and modern written sources; recorded or transcribed speech; judgments by informants that utterances are the same or different, grammatical or ungrammatical; and subsidiary information such as definitions, translational equivalents, and typical situations of use. These are traditional sources of data for working out grammars or parts of grammars, comparative or historical studies, and the like.

Linguists have also turned increasingly to a broader range of data. There is interest in the influence of social variables in dialect studies and their role in historical change. There are studies of bilingualism, and of pidgins and creoles. Anthropological linguists study questions of kinship terminology, folk taxonomy, the ritual use of language, and the functions of language in society. There is research on the instrumental use of language and its relation to situations of use. Questions are raised concerning the psychological capacities and limitations of speakers and listeners, and the relation of speech to the psychological areas of perception, cognition, and concept formation. There is concern with how children learn to speak, and how they continue to learn as adults. In the areas of stylistics, poetics, and the artistic use of language, consideration is given to sentence structure, to the structure and coherence of texts, to devices of parallelism and contrast, to metaphor and other figures, and to questions of prosody. There are studies of discourse in natural conversations in small groups. There is growing interest in variables of pitch, loudness, and vocal quality; in facial expressions and body motion; and in variables of space and distance. Normal speech errors are studied, as are disorders of communication having a neurological, psychological, or developmental origin.

Linguistics, then, has for its de facto observational scope today a broad domain that covers the whole range of human communicative phenomena.

In this whole broad area it has been difficult to bring the observations under the tight control of theory, or sometimes even to accommodate them at all. Thus proposed definitions of the scope of linguistics in terms of the natural scope of any current formal theory are inevitably too limiting, leaving out of account the legitimate observational interests of substantial numbers of linguists. Furthermore, current theory seems to be suffering from other troubles of an internal nature as well.

SCIENCE

Linguists see their discipline as a science. This is a matter of choice, for some of the same data may also be approached philologically or through literary or other studies, which may not necessarily be scientific. Linguistics as a science is thus seen as a program, a way of approaching the data and of trying to gain understanding. The choice of a scientific approach was made at an early date. Rask, for example, in explaining the linguistic approach he was advocating, invoked the names of Linnaeus and Newton (Rask 1830). Schleicher placed linguistics among the natural sciences and carefully distinguished linguistics from philology (1850:1, 1860:119) and from the philosophy of language (1860:119). Bloomfield said that "it is only within the last century or so that language has been studied in a scientific way, by careful and comprehensive observation" (1933:3).

The scientific roots of linguistics stretch back to the ancient Greeks, as is the case for other sciences. A high regard for careful and comprehensive observation was shown by the Alexandrians in the third and second centuries B.C. as they searched for recurrent parallels in texts and worked out grammatical categories. In the same era the Stoics distinguished different levels in grammar by citing as evidence examples of well-formed nonsense and of ambiguity at one level that was resolved at a higher level. Varro, in about 45 B.C., pointed out that in the earlier disputes over analogy and anomaly, both parties deferred to observed usage (*De Lingua Latina* IX 1–3) (Kent 1938).

In modern science the data from observations by the senses are given first place over theory. Theories are inventions or creations of the scientist. They are designed to provide understanding, to interrelate the data in support of a larger picture, and thus to provide insight. Theories in this sense are not wild guesses. They are only proposed with data in view, and they meet their test against data. Theories always remain tentative: when firm observational data collide with the predictions of theory, it is the theory that must give way, no matter how deep our commitment to it may have been.

Theories can be flawed by the incorporation of special assumptions not supported by the data. Such assumptions might be introduced a priori, they might creep in from another discipline, or they might have been inherited through an unquestioned tradition.[1] One problem with unsupported assumptions is that they may mix with the data on which the theory is based, taint the data, and thus obscure our understanding and lead us into error.

Explicit special a priori assumptions can also lead to factionalism and strife. Unsupported by evidence, they can only be maintained by special appeals or the weight of personal authority.[2] This can generate puffery, empty polemics, intellectual bullying, and the great-man syndrome, all symptoms of an unscientific approach. They tend to make it even harder to keep an open mind, for they focus on arguing that someone is right rather than on trying to find out what is right.

Unsupported assumptions inherited from the tradition can be especially troublesome. They are often hidden and overlooked as part of the accepted background and way of thinking we have been taught. Thus they may continue to delude us all. They may lurk in our everyday way of speaking, or even in our technical terminology, and thus they may seem so natural as to be beyond question.

Linguistics has many times uncovered and rejected harmful special assumptions inherited from the tradition and otherwise unsupported. In an earlier era grammars of indigenous languages were often written with undue influence from Latin grammar. The assumption that all languages are structured on a general Indo-European plan, or that the categories of Latin grammar may be universally applicable, has been erased in the best work done today. In order to combat the bias from the school tradition, we take pains to instruct our students in the wide range of exotic features to be found in the languages of the world.

In the last century prescriptivism was thrown out in favor of scientific descriptivism. The scientific linguist was to study what people actually say, not what someone thinks they ought to say. The assumption that language is a prescriptive norm has to be combated, for example when obtaining data from an informant.

Finally recall that linguistics had to discard the Aristotelian assumption of the cross-cultural universality of meanings or mental experience (*On Interpretation* 1). This deeply entrenched assumption conforming to folk theory and common sense had to be challenged and rejected in the light of massive evidence from the comparison of unrelated languages and cultures.

As these examples illustrate, linguistics has acted in the same way as other sciences in trying to discover and remove assumptions and presuppositions unsupported by evidence. In modern science every assumption is open to skepticism and doubt. This is not Cartesian doubt which ends in the acceptance of intuitive truths. It is more like Baconian doubt directed against the idols of the den, of the marketplace, and the others. It is most like Galilean doubt, which meant the suspension of judgment on even traditionally held positions unless and until one has good evidence from the senses or can reason to the conclusion on the basis of good evidence from the senses.

Thus a science works with only a bare minimum of assumptions, building the rest on the solid support of observational evidence. In the more highly developed sciences, the assumptions implicit in the practice of working scientists are of the most general sort. To put it roughly, these are (1) that there is a world out there to be studied, (2) that it is coherent, so we have a chance of finding out something about it, (3) that we can reach valid conclusions by reasoning from valid premises, and (4) that observed effects flow from immediate causes (where there's smoke there's fire).[3]

The question remains, however, whether linguistics is or can become a science in this strong sense. It has been charged, for example, that an approach that advocates the study of linguistic competence is unscientific in that it removes its theories from the possibility of being tested against the observations of actual speech behavior. See Wilks (1972) and Derwing (1973) among others.

Doubts have been raised in some minds as to the legitimacy of linguistics aspiring at all to the status of a science (Robinson 1975:170,182). One can grant to disciplines such as philosophy, philology, or the study of literature the possibility of a nonscientific approach to some of the same phenomena, if that is deemed appropriate by the individuals involved. But in linguistics there is a long-standing and widely accepted goal of approaching the phenomena of interest scientifically. This goal of disciplining the study by scientific methods and principles has mobilized not only the lip service but the deeds of virtually every major linguist since the founding of modern linguistics, and showing that a theory or piece of research is unscientific is still widely seen as the ultimate condemnation of it.

According to this goal, linguistics should adhere to the program and approach of modern science, including particularly that it should build on the accepted foundational assumptions of science referred to previously, that theories must be answerable to observational data, and that any other assumptions unsupported by data, whenever they are discovered, should be rejected.

LANGUAGE

Besides the goal of disciplining its studies by scientific methods and principles, linguistics continues to embrace another long-standing goal. It should study language. Indeed, the discipline is often characterized simply as the scientific study of language.

But what is language? The term is used in a number of senses in everyday language, with which we need not be concerned here. In linguistics there are two major senses. There is the quasi-technical sense where the term is used to refer to the phenomena that are studied in linguistics, or more narrowly, verbal phenomena, texts, and the like. In this sense saying that linguistics is the scientific study of language would say nothing more than that linguistics is the study of certain phenomena of interest, a matter we have already discussed under linguistics. To avoid confusion and to highlight an important distinction, we will continue to use paraphrases for this sense such as linguistic phenomena or communicative phenomena. We will confine our use of the term to its central technical sense whereby language is seen as that which lies behind the phenomena, not the phenomena or data themselves. The goal then simply says that linguistics should study the nature of language as the object lying behind our observations.

What, then, is language? A number of conceptions and definitions have been proposed. But in spite of their differences a common core of agreement can be discerned.

Schleicher, who brought the comparative method to a high degree of development, and was noted for drawing family trees of languages, recognized four parts of grammar: the study of sounds, morphology, the study of function, and syntax (1859). He further distinguished between general grammar and the grammar of particular languages, and between historical linguistics and descriptive linguistics (1860:124–5).[4] Schleicher saw linguistics as a science on a par with other comparative sciences in biology and geology. For him language was an organism like the other organisms of nature—animal, vegetable, and mineral—a kind of fourth kingdom. The term *organism*, which appears to reflect an older animistic view of nature, followed the usage of earlier linguists such as Herder, Wilhelm von Humboldt, and Bopp, and the philosopher Hegel. Schleicher later emphasized that the material basis of language is in the brain and the organs of speech with their nerves, muscles, etc., and that at least at present it is known only through its audible effect in speech (1865).

Whitney (1867:48–51) said that language is an institution—the work of those whose wants it subserves, and in their sole keeping and control. For him it was the product of a series of changes effected by the will and consent of men, but developing in the absence of reflection and conscious intent. He called it a grand system with a highly complicated structure comparable with an organized body. It had its existence only in the minds and mouths of those who use it (1867:35), and it consisted of the associations of ideas and their signs (1867:11).

Saussure, in speaking of language, still used the term *organism* from time to time, but more often he called it a system. According to Saussure, language

is both a social product of the faculty of speech and a collection of necessary conventions that have been adopted by a social body to permit individuals to exercise that faculty. [1916:2;1959:9]

It is a storehouse filled by the members of a given community through their active use of speaking, a grammatical system that has a potential existence in each brain, or, more specifically, in the brains of a group of individuals. For language is not complete in any speaker; it exists perfectly only within a collectivity. [1916:30;1959:13]

It is a system of signs in which the only essential thing is the union of meanings and sound-images, and in which both parts of the sign are psychological. [1916:32;1959:15]

Saussure's view of language as a system of signs has been very influential. Sapir defined language as

a purely human and noninstinctive method of communicating ideas, emotions, and desires by means of a system of voluntarily produced symbols. [1921:8]

This view stresses the idea of communication and appears to focus more on the external symbols produced than on a sign relation existing in the brains of a collectivity. But Sapir goes on to say that

> language . . . consists of a peculiar symbolic relation—physiologically an arbitrary one—between all possible elements of consciousness on the one hand and certain selected elements localized in the auditory, motor, and other cerebral and nervous tracts on the other. . . . Hence, we have no recourse but to accept language as a fully formed functional system within man's psychic or "spiritual" constitution. [1921:10]

He adds that the study of language is

> to be an inquiry into the function and form of the arbitrary systems of symbolism that we term languages. [1921:11]

Here and elsewhere Sapir championed the patterning of language as a system of symbols and its psychological reality.

Leonard Bloomfield (1926) spoke of vocal features or sounds, and stimulus-reaction features of speech. Then by definition an act of speech was an utterance, and the totality of utterances that could be made in a speech-community was the language of that speech-community. A speech-community was defined as a community in which successive utterances are alike or partly alike. The vocal features common to same or partly same utterances were forms, and the corresponding stimulus-reaction features were meanings. The study of sames and differents led in Bloomfield's hands to an inductive method for working out the structure of a language from observational data. He summarized:

> To put it briefly, in human speech, different sounds have different meanings. To study this co-ordination of certain sounds with certain meanings is to study language. [1933:27]

A brief account cannot do full justice to the views of these linguists, but we can elaborate further should it prove necessary. In spite of the obvious differences in these positions, we can see a thread of agreement in what has become the canonical view: language is conceived at once as a relation between sound and meaning, the system or code behind particular utterances or texts, postulated on the basis of evidence and having predictive power, described in terms of grammar and lexicon, and incorporating a series of levels variously understood but typically involving phonology, morphology, syntax, and semantics. This view, in one form or another, is widely, almost universally, held in the discipline today:

> A grammar of a language, in the sense in which I will use this term, can be loosely described as a system of rules that expresses the correspondence between sound and meaning in this language. [Chomsky 1970:52]

A language, by its nature, relates sounds (or graphs, i.e. marks on paper or the like) to meanings. [Lamb 1966:1]

Similar statements from many others could be quoted.

THE DISTINCTION BETWEEN LANGUAGE AND PEOPLE

Contrasting with this canonical view of language and grammar that focuses on a sign relation between sound and meaning and on language as a system of signs, there are other persistent threads where there may be less agreement among various linguists. These are focused not on the system of signs but in some way on the people involved. Since we want to investigate the conceptual structure of linguistics, and we will be discussing such questions as the psychological reality of grammar, the interests of clarity dictate that we carefully distinguish between the conceptual domain of language and the conceptual domain of people, sometimes distinguished in the literature but often curiously confused.

Thus for Schleicher we want to distinguish his view of grammar and the grammars of particular languages and of the parts of grammar, and perhaps his concept of language as an organism or system, from his view of the material basis of language in the brain and the organs of speech.

For Whitney we would distinguish language as a grand system with a highly complicated structure consisting of the association of ideas and their signs, and perhaps his concept of language as an institution, from his concept of its existence in the minds and mouths of those who use it.

For Saussure we would distinguish language as a system of signs uniting meanings and sound-images from its psychological manifestation; the social product of the faculty of speech from the faculty of speech; the collection of conventions from the social body adopting them; and the grammatical system from its existence in the brains of a group of individuals.

For Sapir we would distinguish the system of symbols from its purely human and noninstinctive realization as a method of communicating; language as a peculiar symbolic relation from the elements of consciousness and motor and other cerebrally localized elements; language as a functional system from its existence within man's constitution; and the function and form of arbitrary systems of symbolism from their psychological reality.

For Bloomfield we would distinguish vocal and stimulus-reaction features of speech from the psychological aspects of speakers (which he did not propose to study); the totality of utterances that could be made in a speech-community from the speech-community; and language as the co-ordination of certain sounds with certain meanings, and human speech, from the humans and what they do when they speak and understand.

Thus we will try to maintain a conceptual and terminological separation of language, speech, and grammar from the relevant psychological and social aspects of the real world, whatever they may turn out to be. We will try to eliminate any terminological ambiguity.[5]

It should be noted that our distinction is not between the formal and the informal, or between the abstract and the concrete, or between a theory of something and the thing it is a theory of. Nor is it Saussure's distinction between langue and parole, or the distinction between a grammar and a mechanism for producing and understanding sentences according to the grammar, or the distinction between competence and performance.

Instead we want to distinguish language from the communicative aspects of people; speech or utterances as a product from what people do; and theories in the domain of speech, language, and grammar from theories in the domain of people (Yngve 1981). This distinction has roots in antiquity, as we shall see.

CHAPTER THREE

Analysis:
The Domain of Language

Having made this distinction between language and people, we can now start by examining the first domain: language as a sign relation between sound and meaning given by grammar and lexicon.

THE STATUS OF LANGUAGE

What is the status of language in this sense in linguistics? How are we to understand it? Is it an approach that we adopt as linguists, an optional way of viewing the evidence like the scientific approach? Is it a definite object that can be studied scientifically? Is it an aspect of people (we can now ask), a possession of individuals or of groups? Is it an abstraction or model? Is it a theory based on evidence and subject to test against further data? Is it a special assumption that needs to be examined? All these views and more can be found in the literature.

Saussure appears at first glance to have embraced several of these different views in different places. But in a passage that is perhaps his most important contribution to our present topic, he remarks:

> Other sciences work with objects that are given in advance and that can then be considered from different viewpoints; but not linguistics. . . . Far from it being the object that antedates the viewpoint, it would seem that it is the viewpoint that creates the object. [1916:23;1959:8]

This is not just a passing remark, but something that Saussure had considered very carefully. The critical edition (Engler 1967:24–26) collates a number of columns of his unpublished notes with this single paragraph, and Saussure's point can clearly be seen to mean that other sciences study objects (like rocks, trees, and animals) that are given in advance in that they have an independent external reality and can thus be studied from different points of view. The physical properties of rocks are studied in physics, the chemical properties in chemistry, others in geology, crystallography, and mineralogy. Each science brings its own point of view to the study of the same physical objects, which continue to exist when we move from one order of ideas to another. But the objects of study in linguistics do not have this kind of reality. "Someone pronounces the French word *nu* 'bare'," explains Saussure:

> a superficial observer would be tempted to call the word a concrete linguistic object; but a more careful examination would reveal successively three or four quite different things, depending on whether the word is considered as a sound, as the expression of an idea, as the equivalent of Latin *nudum*, etc. . . . ; besides, nothing tells us in advance that one way of considering the fact in question takes precedence over the others or is in any way superior to them. [1916:23;1959:8]

Saussure is certainly right about this. The objects of language do not have an independent existence of their own; they are actually created by the very point of view taken. Some might object that sound has an external existence of its own. This is true enough, but Saussure answers that trying to reduce language to sound would be to fall into a trap: sound alone would not be speech without the ideas with which it combines. Physical sound, without the linguistic system, is not a linguistic object at all.

Let us consider this point more closely because it contradicts the impression sometimes expressed that the objects of study in linguistics, such as words, meanings, phonemes, formatives, signs, or sentences, are indeed objects that are given in advance like the objects of study in other sciences, or, alternatively, that the objects of study in other sciences, like those in linguistics, are also created by a point of view. The issue concerns the ontological and epistemological status of objects in a science, and the relation of a theory to what it is a theory of.

Let us recall some well-known points regarding how objects are studied in science by taking water as an example. One can observe that water is a colorless liquid and that it freezes and boils. Scientists have measured the temperatures at which it freezes and boils, and how these vary with the pressure. They have measured the volume of one gram of the substance at different temperatures and pressures. They have measured how much light of different wavelengths in the visible, infrared, or ultraviolet portions of the spectrum passes through it at different temperatures and pressures. They have measured how much heat it takes to melt it, to boil it, or to raise its temperature by one degree.

All these measurements, and others, have been compared through the years with a developing body of theory dealing with the properties of water. Properties such as boiling point, melting point, heat of fusion, heat of vaporization, specific heat, density, absorption of light, and others are postulated. These properties are theoretical constructs that enter into tentative theories of water. The theories interrelate the properties and explain them in terms of a larger picture.

The theories are capable of predicting the outcome of further experiments, and this is crucial, for by this means they can be tested against reality and the results can be verified by different scientists in different laboratories, often with different methods. In this way doubts can be resolved and agreement reached. If the predictions are not borne out in careful experiments, the theory may have to be revised. In this way the theory of water has grown and has been integrated into a broader network of physical, chemical, and biological theories. At any point there is a current version of the theory of water, our scientific view of what water is, and there is also the real object water in the real world against which our developing conceptual structure can be tested.

It is the same in other branches of science. For example, concepts of mass, charge, spin, force fields, probability densities, and the like are in the domain of theory subject to testing against careful observations of electrons and their effects in the real world.

The objects of study in linguistics, however, although they are often seen also as having properties as theoretical constructs in a linguistic theory, have no corresponding real objects in the real world against which the theories can be tested. Basically the objects of study in the other sciences are real objects but in linguistics they are not. An elaboration of Saussure's point is that in the other sciences theories can be tested against physical reality; in linguistics they cannot, because there is no corresponding physical reality antedating the viewpoint to test them against. Rather than being objects given in advance that can be studied from a linguistic point of view, they are actually created by the very viewpoint taken.

We can thus conclude that language is not something that can be studied scientifically in any strict sense, for its objects have no independent reality; and it is not an abstraction or model or theory of anything, for there is nothing for it to be an abstraction, model, or theory of. In his unpublished notes Saussure exclaims that the illusion of things *naturally given* in speech is profound. Yes. Linguistic objects still seem very real to us, but it is an illusion. Forgetting this important point can lead us into fallacies, as will shortly become evident.

It is to Bloomfield that we owe a clear recognition of the true status of language in linguistics—the study of language rests on a special assumption.

Bloomfield points out that the individuals in a human society cooperate by means of sound waves which bridge the gap between the nervous systems of speaker and hearer (1933:26,28). Setting aside the mechanisms in the speaker and the hearer as problems for physiology or psychology, he says the linguist deals only with the speech signal (1933:32).

But the study of language can be conducted without special assumptions only so long as we pay no attention to the meaning of what is spoken (1933:75).

This phase of language study is known as *phonetics*. The phonetician finds that no two utterances are exactly alike (1933:76). As long as he ignores the meaning of what is said, he cannot tell us which features are significant for communication and which features are immaterial. A feature which is significant in some languages or dialects may be indifferent in others (1933:77).

Then Bloomfield points out that the difference between distinctive and nondistinctive features of sound lies entirely in the habit of the speakers. In the case of our own language we trust our everyday knowledge to tell us whether speech-forms are "the same" or "different." In the case of a strange language we have to learn such things by trial and error, or to obtain the meanings from someone that knows the language (1933:77).

Then comes a crucial passage:

> The study of *significant* speech-sounds is *phonology* or *practical phonetics*. Phonology involves the consideration of meanings. The meanings of speech-forms could be scientifically defined only if all branches of science, including, especially, psychology and physiology, were close to perfection. Until that time, phonology and, with it, all the semantic phase of language study, rests upon an assumption, the fundamental assumption of linguistics: we must assume that *in every speech-community some utterances are alike in form and meaning.* [1933:78]

Bloomfield discusses this assumption extensively here and in other chapters. On it rests not only phonology but the whole discipline of linguistics.

Bloomfield's assumption is actually a compound of several assumptions. Together they effectively create and introduce into the discipline just those objects of study constituting language that are not given in advance. To understand this, consider that for Bloomfield a *speech-community* is a group of people who use the same system of speech-signals, i.e., the same language (1933:29). Thus, "in every speech-community" introduces by assumption both speech-communities and their languages. An *utterance* is an act of speech, and *alike* reflects judgments of speakers about acts of speech (1926). Thus, "some utterances are alike" introduces by assumption a segmentation not inherent in the sound waves and creates distinguishable units of speech, or speech-sounds. *Forms* are vocal features common to utterances judged the same or partly the same, and the corresponding stimulus-reaction features are *meanings* (1926). Thus, "alike in form and meaning" establishes by assumption that these created units are signs in the traditional sense.

From this we see that Bloomfield's fundamental assumption of linguistics introduces precisely the traditional point of view and creates by assumption the very objects of study in linguistics. Without the assumption we have only the infinitely varying sound waves; with the assumption we have the speech-sounds, forms, and correlated meanings of a language. Without the assumption individuals in a society cooperate by means of sound waves; with the assumption we see them as using a language.

Since language is widely accepted as the domain of study of linguistics, some such assumption, overt or tacit, is widely held in the discipline. Though the phraseology and details of different positions may differ, this assumption lies at the foundation of every grammatical position today. There is no doubt that Saussure and Bloomfield are correct in this matter. The objects constituting language are not given in advance. They are created by a special assumption.

PROBLEMS OF JUSTIFICATION

In a true science all special assumptions are subject to doubt. Is there any scientific justification for an assumption like Bloomfield's creating the objects constituting language? Bloomfield offered no justification. Considering his orientation toward science and his careful use of evidence, this might seem surprising and out of character. He introduced it almost apologetically as a temporary expedient until that time in the future when the other sciences are close to perfection. Perhaps in fact such an assumption cannot be justified. But Bloomfield had been trained in the study of the objects of language, and he and his predecessors and contemporaries viewed their discipline as the study of language. In other words he had received it from a tradition, and in his careful way was only making explicit what had traditionally been assumed.

This tradition, which Robins (1958) called the western grammatical tradition, has been studied extensively by historians of linguistics. Bloomfield himself had reviewed it in the first chapter of *Language* (1933), where he called it simply the study of language. Saussure explicitly acknowledged it when he said that "linguistics, having accorded too large a place to history, will turn back to the static viewpoint of traditional grammar but in a new spirit and with other procedures" (1916:122;1959:82–3). Perhaps if we reexamine from the present point of view the history of this tradition in its several aspects, we can come to understand where an assumption like Bloomfield's might have come from. We may then be able to judge whether or not it has any scientific justification.

The Process View

The history of the study of language can be traced back at least as far as the ancient Greeks. Already in Plato we find historical changes of names treated in terms of adding, transposing, subtracting, or changing letters (*Cratylus* 394 B), an early process view that seems to assume that letters (sounds) are elements of language that can be moved around like counters in a board game.

This view may have come with the development of writing, for what can be written down can easily be objectified, and with alphabetic writing historical change can be observed, reinforcing the idea that there is some *thing* that has changed. It is of interest that a process view is also found in Pāṇini, but this seems not to have appreciably influenced the western tradition until modern times.

A process view has appeared throughout the study of language right up to the present day. The Stoics in the second century B.C. treated barbarism and solecism in similar process terms (Barwick 1922:96–99). Varro in about 45 B.C. treated derivation and inflection (*declinatio*) in process terms (*De Lingua Latina* VI 36, VIII 5,6)(Kent 1938). The fourth century Latin grammarian Donatus treated two modes of barbarism: pronunciation and writing. Under these there were four species: addition, subtraction, change, and transposition, which were applied to letters, syllables, length, accent, and aspiration, giving forty types in all (Keil 1864:392). The spelling tradition has us change *y* to *i* and add *ed*. A process view has been accepted into modern linguistics. We find discussions of syncope, metathesis, ellipsis, and the like (using Greek terms). And we find affix hopping, extraposition, and other transformations.

Whatever its source, whatever the reasons for this objectification, no matter how natural it may have seemed to the ancients or seems to us now, we find no scientific justification here for assuming the elements of language that enter into the process descriptions. And since they are created by a point of view, they have differed in detail according to the different points of view of the different grammarians and linguists involved, thus adding to the confusions and disagreements in the discipline.

THE SEMIOTIC VIEW

In Plato's *Cratylus* we also find concern for the relation of words to their meanings, an early view of a theory of signs. Aristotle is more explicit in *On Interpretation* 1, where we find a remarkably concise statement of the sign relation between written and spoken words, mental experiences, and the things of which our mental experiences are the images.

It was not until the Stoics, however, in the third and second centuries B.C., that a theory of signs, and with it the study of language, was brought together into a coherent doctrine and placed at the very center of philosophy.[1] The Stoics divided philosophy into three parts: physical, logical, and ethical. The logical part, which contained dialectic and rhetoric, was central, for without it physics and ethics could not express themselves. Stoic dialectic was in fact a highly developed philosophical theory of knowledge, a sophisticated elaboration of Aristotle's theory of signs. It related signifier, signified, and referent through a series of levels of representation from *phōnē* 'sound' through *lexis* 'diction' and *logos* 'speech' to *lekton*, the highly developed logical deep structure or meaning that was the signified, and from this through levels of perception and sensation to real objects, the referents in the real world. Stoic grammar by 150 B.C. already had a distinctly modern look. The grammar comprised three of the levels: sound (a phonetic level), diction (a phonological and phonotactic level), and speech (a grammatical and syntactic level). Three of the parts of speech—the proper noun, common noun, and verb—were defined in terms of what they signified at the logic or lekton level. These were individual qualities like *Diogenes*, *Socrates*; general qualities like *man*, *horse*; and isolated predicates like *write*, *speak*. The other two parts of speech were defined grammatically and syntactically.

The whole structure of Stoic dialectic, of which their grammar was but a part, focused on how one knows the truth about referents in the real world in terms of logical propositions, and how these are signified by vocal sounds that can be written down. In this the criterion of truth was the apprehending presentation, that which comes from a real object, agrees with that object itself, and has been imprinted on the mind—and is conveyed through the senses. Epistemology has made changes and advances since the Stoics, but in modern science we still test our theories of what is true about the world by applying observational criteria.

When normative grammar grew out of Stoic dialectic it did not carry over the propositional-logic level of lekton nor the levels of perception and sensation. Some of the parts of speech, however, were still defined partially in terms of what they signified at a logic or meaning level. Thus the theory-of-signs idea of language as a relation between sound and meaning given by grammar and lexicon was retained in normative grammar. We find such a treatment and definitions in the works of the second-century grammarian Apollonius Dyscolus, in the grammar usually attributed to Dionysius Thrax, in the early Latin grammars of Donatus and Priscian, and in the various grammars of European nationalism right up to modern times. Meanwhile the theory of signs was kept alive by philosophers to whom epistemology and the theory of knowledge were of special interest. Although modern linguistics has moved away from prescriptivism, it has generally retained the ancient intellectual standpoint. Grammarians and linguists who have read the classics or the writings of philosophers and logicians have been able to rediscover there the ancient theory that had always been implicit in grammatical writings, particularly in the familiar traditional definitions of the parts of speech, the form-meaning organization of dictionaries, and the standard definition of language as a relation between sound and meaning. Thus to many the theory of signs, when encountered for the first time, has seemed eminently natural and inevitable. To others, however, it has seemed strange and counterintuitive.

Although this semiotic view of language is widely held among modern linguists, as we have seen, and Stoic grammar as a precursor of modern linguistics has been acknowledged by Jakobson (1965), Sebeok (1974), and others, still we cannot find a scientific justification here for assuming objects conceived as signs. In fact, in a theory of knowledge, signs and their sounds and meanings are explicitly not objects given in advance that can be studied through the senses like the objects of study of the other sciences. They are not objects in the real world at all. They are treated not as objects to be known scientifically but rather as part of the means of knowing.

We have to conclude that we do not find here a scientific justification for an assumption of signs as objects of study in linguistics. Furthermore the ancient semiotic standpoint has certain disabilities as a foundation for a modern scientific linguistics. In the first place a philosophical or theory-of-knowledge concern for expressing the truth, if it actually is a concern of modern linguistics, is much too narrow a standpoint. It leaves out of account the many other presumed uses of language mentioned earlier as being of interest in modern linguistics. Designed for a narrow philosophical purpose, the theory is ill-suited as a foundation for treating issues in the broader domain, for example topics in pragmatics. Second, the focus on truth in a theory of knowledge has tended to take as the standard case one word one meaning and unambiguous propositions independent of context. This has raised the problem of ambiguity, for everywhere we find utterances depending heavily on the situational context, and the theory is not equipped to handle the situational context. These points and some of their consequences will be elaborated further in a later section.

THE TEXT-BASED VIEW

The Alexandrians in the third and second centuries B.C. had a somewhat different approach to grammar. Their concerns were Homeric studies, rejuvenating poetry, organizing knowledge, and preserving the great literary heritage of the past (Pfeiffer 1968; Sandys 1915). From this effort came text-based methods in grammar and literary criticism which involved, for example, collecting all the parallels in the *Iliad* and *Odyssey*. Aristophanes of Byzantium worked out recurrent patterns of inflection, stated general rules of analogy, paid attention to current spoken dialects of Greek, and tried to preserve and indicate the original pronunciation in the reading of ancient poetry by inventing special diacritics and inserting them in texts to indicate accent and quantity. Aristarchus of Samothrace recognized eight parts of speech (Quintilian, *Inst.Orat.* I iv 18–20)(Watson 1856), and is credited with adding a sixth rule of analogy to the five of Aristarchus (Barwick 1925:149). The rules of analogy provided tests for classifying words:

If two words were of the same 'kind', *e.g.* both of them nouns or verbs in the
same 'case' or 'inflection', and identical in termination, number of syllables and
sound, they were 'analogous' to one another; *i.e.* they belonged to the same
declension or conjugation. [Sandys 1915:50–1]

According to the sixth test, both words were to be simple or both compound.
One can see here the forerunner of modern text-based methods, including the
methods of sames and differents. However, we still do not find here any
justification for assuming that the objects compared are given in advance in
any scientific sense.

THE NORMATIVE VIEW

The normative tradition, lasting two millennia from the time of the Stoics,
had considerable influence on the conception of language and grammar, a
point to which we will return in a later section. In connection with the present
topic, however, it should be noted that a prescriptive norm would likely be
perceived by speakers and writers as something external to them, something
out there that is powerful and has to be dealt with and reacted to, thus en-
hancing the illusion that language is a concrete reality with a natural existence
or "life" of its own.[2] We could investigate scientifically how or why people
may perceive language as an external reality. But of course their perception,
belief, intuition, or illusion, even if it were universal, or even innate, could
not be taken as a scientific justification for an assumption creating the objects
of language or language itself.

THE HYPOTHETICAL CONSTRUCT VIEW

What about the many linguistic insights that have been obtained within frameworks assuming the objects of language? Perhaps there is a justification here:
call the assumption a hypothesis supported and strengthened by all those
valuable results. But recall also the many problems facing linguistics with
which we started. The prognosis under the current regimen does not seem
very hopeful. Besides, it is not sufficient for a body of theory to be adequate,
say, 80 percent of the time. Applications of the traditional Latin grammatical
categories to indigenous languages in previous centuries also gave some worthwhile results; the grammars are still useful even today. But that wasn't sufficient. The theory failed in various respects and thus had to be discarded.

Perhaps the objects of language are hypothetical constructs, theoretical
entities postulated to account for the evidence. Language would then be in
the realm of theory. The trouble with this is that there is nothing for language
in this sense to be a theory of. True, grammar is often taken to be in the
realm of theory—a theory of language—but this does not help, for as we have
seen, the objects of language, such as speech-sounds, phonemes, syllables,

morphemes, words, phrases, sentences, meanings, sememes, signs, or others, are not objects naturally given and existing independently of theory.

THE LACK OF JUSTIFICATION

Careful search has not turned up a scientific justification for an assumption creating the objects of language. These objects are not given in advance, but created by a point of view, as Saussure once realized, and their introduction into linguistics requires a special assumption, as Bloomfield emphasized.

An inability to justify special claims or foundational assumptions on the basis of solid evidence is the criterion by which science has rejected all sorts of false theories, mistaken ideas, erroneous superstitions, unwarranted speculation, and rampant mysticism. In all such cases the burden of providing justification rests on those who would continue to maintain the assumption or theory. It must be this way; otherwise science would be led to accept all sorts of guesses, hunches, and wild ideas that could not be justified. Without proper justification how do we know that it makes any more sense to have a science that studies the objects of language than it would to have a biology of unicorns, griffins, and chimeras even if we *had* found tracks in the mud by the river bank?

It is sometimes suggested that Bloomfield's assumption, though admittedly false, should be retained anyway, since it has proved fruitful in stimulating research: "Ask of a theory, 'What has it done for me lately?' " An argument like this could be used to perpetuate any false lead that had turned up clues. Better that we should seek the truth than preserve past delusions. Science is tolerant of hypotheses in their early stages and tries to find evidence for their truth or falsity. But when a hypothesis proves to be unfounded it must be abandoned forthwith lest it misdirect our research and distort our understanding of nature.

If Bloomfield's assumption or its equivalent cannot be justified, which appears to be the case, a linguistics based on the assumption cannot be a science. Note that this is true independently of what may have been the origin of the assumption, its history, or its sometime intuitive appeal. Without adequate scientific justification by evidence from the senses, it is a special assumption over and above the minimum assumptions of all science, and therefore it has no place in science.

Thus we see that with the usual conception of language and the objects of language, and the standard conception of science based on observation and theory, the frequently expressed definition of linguistics as the scientific study of language is an oxymoron. It involves a contradiction in terms. There is no hope of having a linguistics of language that is scientific. The two goals of linguistics, that it study language and that it be a science, are incompatible.

But business as usual in linguistics has accepted these two incompatible goals. It might be urged that we should continue to accept both goals, that there are benefits in retaining inconsistent theories, and besides, we have nothing better. But the benefits of inconsistent theories are illusory, and there are at least two alternatives, one of which will be examined in some detail in later chapters. A linguistics governed by business as usual is living on borrowed time. Simple intellectual honesty dictates that we recognize that the goal of studying language is incompatible with the goal that linguistics be a science, and business as usual, in accepting both goals, is incoherent. Besides, if we ask what this position has done for us lately, we would have to say that it has led us astray. It has led to the chaotic proliferation of inevitably inadequate grammatical theories.

Thus it appears that we cannot properly continue with business as usual. There is a fork in the road ahead. Either we can have a linguistics of language that retains Bloomfield's assumption or its equivalent and cannot be a science, or we can have a scientific linguistics, in which case we will have to give up Bloomfield's assumption. We cannot have it both ways.

On the first alternative, linguistics would study language and be disciplined by grammar. Resting ultimately on assumptions, it would relinquish the possibility of testing central aspects of its theory against reality. When theories differed in these aspects there would be no objective criteria for choosing among them. Under this alternative, linguistics would not be a science in the strict sense even if it continued to call itself a science.

On the second alternative the phenomena identified above in the section on linguistics would be studied scientifically. Linguistics would be disciplined by science. But without the assumption of the objects of language, the theoretical structure of linguistics would have to be rebuilt. This could be a large undertaking.

We must choose one or the other of these incompatible alternatives: that linguistics should retain its goal of studying language, or that it should retain its goal of being a science.

CHAPTER FOUR

Analysis:
The Domain of People

Having examined the domain of speech, language, and grammar, we now turn to the other domain, the domain focusing in some way on people, individually and collectively.

EXPLANATIONS IN TERMS OF PEOPLE

An adequate understanding of linguistic phenomena has long been seen as requiring an analysis ultimately in terms of psychological and social realities. Thus in addition to the incompatible goals of linguistics that it should study language and that it should be a science, there is a third goal, sometimes acknowledged, not always accepted, that linguistics should seek explanations in terms of people. There are a number of examples in the history of linguistics where explanations in terms of people have been proposed. Let us review a few.

In classical antiquity Plato had Socrates say that the original words have been completely buried by those who wished to dress them up, and that the inserting of extra letters in words is the work of people who care nothing for the truth, but only for the shape of their mouths (*Cratylus* 414 B-E). Varro explained the function of grammatical processes such as derivation and inflection as saving people from having to memorize a large vocabulary in toto (*De Lingua Latina* VIII 4–7)(Kent 1938). Thus he said that new slaves introduced into a large household could quickly inflect the names of all their fellow slaves in the oblique cases, provided only that they had heard the nominative.

In the earlier period of modern linguistics the relations between language families worked out by the comparative method were interpreted in terms of the wanderings of peoples from one place to another, carrying their language with them. For example, Fick (1871:1045ff) tried to work out their itinerary in geographic and temporal detail. Or the data were interpreted in terms of an original gradation or continuum of dialects in which regional languages grew up by neighboring people adopting the way of speaking of prestige centers (Schmidt 1872). Changes were seen in terms of people making analogies, a point emphasized by the neogrammarians. Or observed changes were seen as due to problems in communication caused by homonyms resulting from sound change (Gilliéron and Roques 1912). Or the rate of change was seen as related to the actual density of communication among speakers (Bloomfield 1933:326,340).

In more recent years there have been investigations of the social motivation of sound change (Labov 1963), and of the social factors responsible for speakers alternating between different styles or different languages (Gumperz 1962). It has been hypothesized that the properties of human temporary memory are related causally to language structure and language change (Yngve 1960). Hall (1962) has seen a creole as developing when a pidgin acquires native speakers. Naro (1978) has traced the origin of pidgin Portuguese partly to native speakers of West African languages being captured, taken to Portugal, and there taught Portuguese so they could be used as translators. Silverstein (1972) has offered an interpretation of Chinook Jargon as a drastically reduced form of each speaker's primary language so that each speaker in speaking it may retain his own syntactic base. These are just a few of the many attempts to understand the observed phenomena in terms of the realities of people and what they do, that is, in terms of psychological and social realities.

There have been continued calls for linguistics to turn away from the domain of language and concern itself more with the domain of people. When modern scientific linguistics started, it was seen as part of the natural history of man (Rask, Bopp, Schleicher, and others). The neogrammarians in their manifesto pointed out that language is not a thing which leads a life of its own outside of and above human beings, but that it has its true existence only in the individual, and hence all changes in the life of language can only proceed from the individual speaker. It was not the Greek language which dropped final *t*, but those among the Greeks with whom the sound change started (Osthoff and Brugman 1878:xii)(Lehmann 1967:204,209). Hermann Paul stated the program of linguistics as

> showing how the single individual is related to the community; receiving and giving; defined by the community and defining it in turn; and how the younger generation enters on the heritage of the elder. [1889:xxx]

But Saussure said that linguistics has accorded too large a place to history and must turn back to grammar. Nevertheless he placed langue in the minds of a collectivity as had linguists before him.

As linguistics turned back to grammar, Sapir pointed out that:

> it is peculiarly important that linguists, who are often accused, and accused justly, of failure to look beyond the pretty patterns of their subject matter, should become

aware of what their science may mean for the interpretation of human conduct in general. Whether they like it or not, they must become increasingly concerned with the many anthropological, sociological, and psychological problems which invade the field of language. [1929:214]

Gardiner (1932:6) spoke of the crisis of grammar, and proposed to try to find out how speech works by putting back single acts of speech into their original setting of real life. Malinowski saw that linguists were faced by a dilemma.

Once we recognize . . . that "language is a form of activity, a mode of human behavior, perhaps the most important," the question arises: Can we treat language as an independent subject of study? Is there a legitimate science of words alone, of phonetics, grammar, and lexicography? Or must all study of speaking lead to sociological investigation, to the treatment of linguistics as a branch of the general science of culture? [1937:172]

But Bloomfield abandoned his earlier reliance on psychology and criticized Hermann Paul for accompanying

his statements about language with a paraphrase in terms of mental processes which the speakers are supposed to have undergone. The only evidence for these mental processes is the linguistic process; they add nothing to the discussion, but only obscure it. [1933:17]

Bloomfield's influence was on the side of moving linguistics back to the study of speech, language, and grammar, and away from the study of people.

More recently, there have been calls for developing an ethnography of speaking (Hymes 1962), and for linguistics to concentrate on investigating how people use language to communicate (Yngve 1969). Sociolinguists have increasingly tried to focus on people interacting in social groups, but Chomsky has reiterated his position of idealizing away from people and social groups. His concept of competence represents a move back to the domain of language and grammar, although competence is supposed to exist in the head of the native speaker.

Not only have explanations been given in terms of people, but actually all the data for linguistics, without exception, also stem from people. Recall that the observational domain of linguistics today covers the whole broad range of human communicative phenomena.

At least since the beginning of modern scientific linguistics, the issue of the two domains has been with us, the one concerned with speech, language, and grammar, the other concerned with people and the psychological and social reality. The interrelationships of these domains, their clashes, and our confusions continue to be debated widely. The question of which should be dominant continues as an underlying theme in the linguistics literature, where it is conceived in terms of current conceptions of grammar. For example, there is the current issue of whether or not people actually carry out transformations when they speak. Or, more generally, do they in speaking execute grammar rules of any sort, or are these to be seen as part of some different domain? We tend to forget that this is just the current version of a very old question.

THE FALLACIES OF THE PSYCHOLOGICAL AND SOCIAL REALITY OF GRAMMAR

In spite of the many calls to focus on people instead of on language, and in spite of the widely acknowledged need for explanations in terms of people, we find that essentially all linguistic thought directed toward the domain of people has actually been put forth in terms of language and grammar.

Plato, when he talked about people caring more for the shapes of their mouths than for the truth, was talking in terms of changes of letters (sounds) and names using the current concepts in the domain of speech and language. Varro, in talking about slaves not having to learn separately all the inflected forms of names, spoke in the grammatical terms of nominative and oblique cases. The neogrammarians in their manifesto spoke about some among the Greeks dropping final *t* when the sound change started. Gardiner wanted to put back the single acts of speech into their original setting of real life, but ended up talking about words, meanings, sentences, and the like. Yngve discussed a model hypothesized to represent a speaker in some respects, including a mechanism and permanent and temporary memory organs, but the permanent memory was populated with a grammar, and the mechanism moved symbols representing grammatical entities into and out of the temporary memory as it produced grammatical sentences. And Chomsky talked about the competence of the native speaker, but ended up discussing his current version of transformational-generative grammar, which was then supposed to underlie performance in some way, although its relation to performance, he now says, is not just a problem but a real mystery.

We have attempted to focus on people, on a psychological and social reality, but the phenomena have been interpreted in terms of language and grammar. We have looked at people but have seen speech-sounds, forms, and meanings. Instead of people we have seen parts of speech, sentences, paradigms, rules, and the rest. This has required the introduction of unsupported assumptions to create the objects of language and grammar, the assumptions constituting Bloomfield's fundamental assumption of linguistics or its equivalent. Then, since we are interested in explanations in terms of people, the grammatical results have been reinterpreted in terms of people. This has required the introduction of further assumptions, that grammar has a psychological reality and a social reality, that is, that grammar has an existence in the physical domain. Such assumptions are fallacies.

Let us look more closely at what has happened.

First we have looked at people in terms of language and grammar: the observations in linguistics, every one of them, are actually observations of people, but the usually tacit assumptions creating the traditional objects of language and grammar have interposed themselves between our eyes and the phenomena. Thus the linguistic results flow in fact not only from the data but also from the assumptions. Since the assumptions are unjustified, the results are thereby insecure. It is difficult to know to what extent they flow from the observations and to what extent they flow from the assumptions. The results may seem coherent and may even be able to predict other observations. They may even appear to be adequate, say, 80 percent or more of the time, thus increasing our confidence in them and reinforcing an idea that linguistics is an empirical science, and that we are on the right track. But the widely held perceptions of adequate empirical support for linguistic results are a mistake if unsupported assumptions have also been accepted. We know from our experience with Latin grammar applied to indigenous languages that a theory based on inappropriate and unsupported assumptions can appear to be adequate in many respects, yet be unacceptable in the end. To the extent that the unsupported assumptions creating the objects of language and grammar adversely affect the results, we will experience serious problems of adequacy. And to the extent that different linguists proceed on the basis of somewhat different assumptions, they may achieve different areas of apparent adequacy, and there may be areas where their claims stand in conflict. Such unsupported assumptions represent an a priori, arbitrary, and nonempirical or untestable component at the very heart of the discipline, leading to conflicting views of language, endless argumentation, and lack of convergence on scientifically adequate results.

Then, second, in order to achieve understanding in terms of people, the resulting grammar is thrust into the head of native speakers or predicated of the community in some way. This requires a second set of assumptions: that grammar has a psychological and a social reality. On these assumptions, objects in the domain of language, which have no external existence independent of theory, but are based instead on a priori assumptions, are reified—given a reality in the real world—a psychological or social reality. There is a psychological reality, and a social reality, but to identify either or both of these with language in the technical sense of a sign relation between sound and meaning given by grammar and lexicon is a fallacy. It is a category mistake of the most serious kind: they exist in different domains altogether.

Furthermore, the results in the domain of language and grammar are already unsteady, since they rest in part on the unsupported assumptions creating the objects of language and grammar.

Thus the goal that linguistics should seek explanations in terms of people is incompatible with the goal that linguistics should study language.

THE GRIP OF THE TRADITION

In spite of the many plausible explanations in terms of people and the extreme scarcity of reasonable explanations in terms of language alone, theories of language and grammar still hold sway. As an interesting side issue one may speculate as to the reasons for this continued preoccupation with the objects of speech, language, and grammar. First, the extensive teaching of traditional grammar in the schools for more than two millennia has assured these ancient ideas a continuing place on the intellectual landscape instead of their being discarded.[1] Second, the continued interest of philosophers in logic and epistemology has often turned their attention to concepts of language in a theory of signs, thus keeping this aspect of the tradition alive. Third, the theory of language and grammar has been the most highly developed body of theory in the whole area, the most successful in dealing with complexity and detail, and might be expected to preempt the field for this reason alone. Fourth, no good alternative has been available even for those who have been dissatisfied with current theory. Fifth, most of the technical linguistic concepts available, such as morpheme, meaning, vowel, sentence, and the like are defined in terms of language and grammar, so any careful thinking in the area tends to bring in the preconceptions of this theoretical structure. And sixth, the related familiar concepts available in everyday language similarly have their meaning in the realm of words, language, meaning, and the like. Consequently it has been very difficult to think clearly in the domain centered on people without being drawn into the ancient conceptual structure and terminology of speech, language, and grammar—the Sapir-Whorf hypothesis in action.

The psychological and social reality of grammar fallacies are inherent in present conceptions of linguistic study. They follow nearly automatically from the course of development of scientific linguistics in the last century and a half. First there was the demand of science for careful observation and the basing of etymologies and statements of language change on solid observational evidence rather than on free speculation or philosophical preconceptions. Then there was the scientific demand for the accountability of theory to the evidence, which required increased explicitness and formalization in the theory so as to relate to the details of observation. This naturally led to further developing and improving the already highly developed traditional grammatical theory, an effort of approximately the last hundred years. Finally there was the demand of science for understanding and explanation, and the realization that explanations must ultimately relate to people. When grammatical theory is linked to efforts at understanding in terms of people, the fallacies arise. This is undoubtedly the reason that Bloomfield a half century ago tried to draw away from explanations in terms of people. But the demands for explanations in terms of people remain and even seem to have been increasing, bringing the fallacies ever more into play and exposing to view many confusing and difficult problems in the discipline.

But whether these speculations are correct or not, it is evident, in conclusion, that trying to interpret observations of people in terms of language and grammar and then trying to understand people indirectly in terms of language and grammar is injurious to our attempts to achieve a scientific understanding. It involves an unjustified assumption of the objects of language and grammar. It thus interposes an inappropriate theoretical structure between our observations of people and our understanding of people. It leads to a reliance on arbitrary or a priori criteria for judging statements that cannot be tested against evidence from the senses, and thus it tends to lead us into empty polemics and endless argumentation. And it leads us into the psychological and social reality of grammar fallacies. In these ways it frustrates our efforts to erect an adequate linguistic science.

Indeed, many of the current difficulties in the discipline mentioned earlier can be seen as expected symptoms of this underlying conceptual problem in the foundations of linguistics—the fact that the goal of linguistics to study language, which is incompatible with its goal to be a science, is also incompatible with its goal to seek explanations in terms of people.

CHAPTER FIVE

Implications

What are the implications of this analysis, finally, for viewing the current and historical context of the choice we face?

THE TWO DOMAINS

The distinction between the domain of speech, language, and grammar on the one hand, and the domain of people, individually and collectively, on the other, is perhaps clear by now. It is a distinction that had its origin in antiquity. The Stoic split at the most basic level of philosophy between the the logical part and the physical separated the topics of dialectic and rhetoric in the logical part from biological, medical, and other topics, including the eight parts of the (material) psyche or soul, in the physical part (Diogenes Laertius VII 39–47, 132–3, 157–9). It thus separated the study of speech and language from the study of sound as vibrations in the air. It separated sensation and perception as part of how we know the truth from the five senses as parts of the psyche. It separated logic and the form of argument from the power of reasoning as part of the psyche. And most important, it separated language and grammar from the power of speech as another part of the psyche. Thus it separated the perceptual, logical, and grammatical as parts of a theory of knowledge from the physical and psychological as parts of the real world.

It is usual even today to separate the phonological from the phonetic, the logical from the psychological, and the epistemological and philosophical from the biological, chemical, and physical. The choice between a grammatical linguistics and a scientific linguistics is basically a choice between these two domains. It is a choice between a linguistics that sees itself in terms of concepts of language and grammar as part of the philosophical domain of logic, epistemology, and the theory of knowledge, and a linguistics that seeks to understand the phenomena within its purview as natural phenomena, as aspects of physical reality to be studied scientifically.

The nature of this choice may have been partly concealed from the founders of modern scientific linguistics because the very powerful tradition of nor-

mative grammar had intervened historically, and the choice between the traditional and the scientific was then seen in terms of a choice between fanciful
and well-supported etymologies, between normative and descriptive grammars, between grammars grounded in logic and grammars grounded on usage,
and between grammars influenced by Latin grammar or the native language
of the linguist and grammars true to the languages being described. In each
case the traditional philosophically based concepts of language and grammar
remained assumed and not brought into question.

The Stoics also saw and discussed important issues in the conduct of investigation in the two domains. Their theory of dialectic provided a criterion
of truth about physical reality. The criterion was evidence through the senses,
and on this they agreed. But they also asked what we would see as a metatheoretical question. What criterion of truth could be used in studying incorpo-
real things like the objects of logic? They faced this question by allowing
also a nonapprehending presentation, which was received not through the
senses, but through the mind itself or through reason. But this way of knowing
was more controversial with them, some appealing to right reason, others to
innate ideas or gifts of nature (Diogenes Laertius VII 46, 49–54). Even today
there is wide agreement in philosophy that the appropriate criterion of truth
in the scientific study of nature in the physical domain is ultimately evidence
from the senses, but there continue to be disagreements about what criteria
of truth are appropriate in the logical or metatheoretical domain, for example
the disputes between empiricism and rationalism. The issue of what criterion
of truth can be used when tests against physical reality are impossible is still
a nagging concern in linguistics and the subject of a rapidly proliferating
literature. It has no satisfactory answer short of insisting that theories be
testable against a physical reality.

Modern science has prospered by focusing on the physical, where evidence
can be obtained through the senses, and trying to reduce to a minimum any
assumptions in the logical, philosophical, or metaphysical domain that cannot
be tested against evidence from the senses. If assumptions can be introduced
freely without empirical support, then anyone can introduce any convenient
fictions that he thinks may be plausible, and when such assumptions conflict
there are no reliable criteria for choosing among them. Witness the well-
known nonuniqueness of phonemic solutions of phonetic systems. The endless
march of new types of grammar cannot be expected to converge on a satisfactory agreed-upon body of linguistic theory, for as we saw, there are no
real objects for them to be a theory of and against which they can be tested.[1]
Compare the point made in a philosophical context by Hutchinson (1974:72)
that in a ''descriptive'' (nonmental) linguistics, grammatical theory cannot
be empirically true, as there is nothing for it to be true of. We would have

to add that grammatical theory in a mental linguistics founders on the psychological reality of grammar fallacy.

Bloomfield's analysis appears to be an attempt to isolate explicitly in a single fundamental assumption all the nonempirical factors in linguistics not shared with the more highly developed sciences. This may have been an attempt to move linguistics toward science, but the assumption certifies its nonscientific nature at the very core. The recent rationalistic trend in linguistics under the stimulus of Noam Chomsky and others has actually increased rather than decreased the nonempirical content of proposed linguistic theories, which would move linguistics still further away from science. It is significant that philosophers themselves have recognized Chomsky's theories as being more in the realm of philosophy than of empirical science, no matter how Chomsky himself may have represented them (Ringen 1975; Botha 1971, 1973).

The problem associated with the psychological and social reality of grammar fallacies is an epistemological problem—the attempt to explain aspects of objects in the physical domain, people, which can be studied by evidence obtained through the senses, in terms of theories of the assumed immaterial objects of language in the logical domain, which are not given in advance, cannot be observed through the senses, and in fact have to be introduced by a special assumption, created out of whole cloth, as it were.

Basically it is a question of levels of theory and metatheory. On the first alternative facing linguistics, theory would be at the metatheoretical level as developed by the ancients and elaborated through philosophy and normative grammar. Its objects of study would inevitably be introduced by assumption. On the second alternative, linguistic theory would be at the lower level of scientific theory and would study real objects. It would accept only the standard metatheoretical assumptions of modern science. A linguistics that inappropriately confuses the two levels by trying to accept both grammar and science is incoherent and contains serious fallacies.

It is ironic that grammar and the theory of signs, originating in ancient epistemology, should lead to epistemological problems when assumed as the theoretical foundation of modern linguistics. The fact that linguistics has made the progress that it has in spite of this handicap is a tribute to the philosophers, grammarians, and linguists involved. But if linguistics is to be a science, it cannot accept in its foundations any assumptions like Bloomfield's fundamental assumption of linguistics.

We will finally have to choose between a philosophical linguistics and a scientific linguistics, that is, between a grammatical linguistics that studies language in the logical domain and cannot be scientific, and a scientific linguistics that studies the phenomena as aspects of nature in the physical domain, for efforts to do both at the same time are incoherent and lead to fallacies.

It is important to understand that the choice facing the discipline between the first alternative, the second alternative, and business as usual is of an entirely different order from the familiar problem of choosing between different approaches to grammar.

It is difficult to choose decisively among the many forms of grammar because they differ basically in the details of the assumptions they accept, and since the assumptions cannot be justified in any case by evidence from the senses, there is a rather large amount of arbitrariness involved. Thus arguments over the relative advantages of various positions are often inconclusive. Choices are often made instead on such extrinsic grounds as aesthetic considerations, allegiance to a school of thought, or familiarity with a particular position through accidents of schooling or training. Positions are sometimes maintained or defended by polemics and the personal authority of charismatic individuals who adopt an eclipsing stance. As a reaction against this exclusionary atmosphere, there has grown up in some quarters an ethic of tolerance for conflicting positions. A linguist can even hedge or waffle on his choice of theory, eclectically selecting a bit from here and a bit from there, and in this way new positions are often born.

But the choices with which we are concerned here are quite different. They are substantive choices allowing no middle ground or compromise. This may appear to some to conflict with the ethic of tolerance and eclecticism. But the whole point of science is to be able to find objective reproducible criteria for making choices. Scientific tolerance of a plurality of hypotheses stands in proportion to their reasonableness and the lack of scientific evidence suggesting their falsity.

The choice between business as usual and one of the alternatives is a choice between an inherently incoherent linguistics that contains fallacies and an alternative that has a chance of being coherent and free of fallacies. To choose a coherent position over an incoherent position cannot be seen as arbitrarily exclusionary. It is hard to conceive of a good reason to retain an incoherent position, and it is doubtful that it could be shown convincingly that business as usual is not incoherent.

The choice between the two coherent alternatives is a choice between two quite different sorts of linguistics. It is a choice between a philosophical linguistics and a scientific linguistics.

THE TWO COHERENT ALTERNATIVES

Let us consider what linguistics would look like under each of these alternatives, and examine some of the most obvious advantages and disadvantages of each.

A GRAMMATICAL LINGUISTICS

Under the first alternative, linguistics would be disciplined by grammar and would study the objects of language. It would eliminate the incompatibility with the scientific goal by turning its back on any aspirations to be scientific, and it would avoid the psychological and social reality of grammar fallacies by setting aside the goal of seeking explanations in terms of people. It would take the concept of grammar literally to its logical conclusion, a pure grammar associated with a pure logic in the first domain. And following the lead of many logicians and prescriptive grammarians, it would carefully distinguish itself from the merely psychological and from the faulty logic and careless speech of ordinary people. If the predictions from an assumed logical principle, grammatical norm, or Platonic ideal conflicted with what people are actually observed to do, this alternative would resolutely place theory over observation, for to allow theory to be corrected by observation, if consistently followed, would inevitably lead to rejecting the foundational assumptions of the first alternative and thereby move the discipline to the second alternative, since as we have seen, a coherent discipline cannot follow both alternatives at the same time.

This alternative has the not inconsiderable advantage of being hooked into a very long grammatical, logical, and philosophical tradition with a familiar and highly developed conceptual structure. A rather large literature already exists within this tradition that can support further research. With support from this strong background, only a few years are needed to produce a new version of grammar. It also embodies a conceptual structure related to normative grammar and to the folk theory familiar to the public. Thus advances in a linguistics of this sort might be more readily applicable to improving normative grammar and the traditional teaching of composition, foreign languages, and other communicative arts and skills through grammar (although the efficacy of teaching these skills through grammar is sometimes disputed).

A major disadvantage of this alternative is one that it shares with current linguistic theory. It incorporates a foundation of unsupported assumptions. To the extent that theoretical statements rest in part on these unsupported assumptions, they are untestable. There are no objective criteria for accepting or rejecting them. This leaves us with nothing more substantial than dogma or opinion in the more central and basic regions of linguistic theory. If different linguists hold to different sets of assumptions, there are no objective criteria for deciding among them. There is thus a temptation to resort to polemics, imposition of authority, arbitrary dicta, and appeals to simplicity, symmetry of patterning, elegance, personal revelation, or other sorts of inconclusive argumentation. Such unresolvable differences have already fractionated the discipline into camps or schools of thought, reducing the cooperative nature of the discipline by making it difficult or impossible to compare results. This has led to wasted effort as each camp reworks linguistic theory to suit itself. This disadvantage is connected with the incompatibility of this alternative with a goal to be scientific.

Another disadvantage of this first alternative is associated with the necessity that it relinquish the goal of seeking explanations in terms of people. It lacks contact with reality. Its relation, if any, to the observations and data of linguistics is tenuous and problematic at best. It provides poor or no support for primarily observational research and little or no insight into what may lie behind the data. Thus it is incapable of serving the functions of a scientific theory.

A pure grammatical discipline according to the first alternative is possible, but in abandoning the quest for a scientific understanding of the phenomena, it would reverse a century and a half effort to develop a scientific linguistics and go against the long-established historical trend of particular sciences crystallizing out of philosophy. It would make linguistics either a part of philosophy, a part of the normative arts, or both. This would be a position true to its origin in Stoic thought, but whether a discipline of this sort would be appropriate as a part of philosophy today is for one or another of the schools of philosophy to decide. It is not appropriate for linguistics. It could not provide adequate theoretical underpinnings for confronting the observations of interest in linguistics previously identified. Whether it is more suitable for application in the normative and practical arts than an approach through the second alternative is a separate issue, and one that cannot yet be decided one way or the other.

A SCIENTIFIC LINGUISTICS

Under the second alternative, linguistics would be disciplined by science rather than by grammar. But if we give up studying the traditional objects of language, of grammar, and of a sign relation between sound and meaning, because they are only created by a point of view, what objects are there for linguistics to study that do actually exist independently of theory and can be studied scientifically? There can be no other answer than people, individually and in groups—the people who communicate. They are the source of our data and the locus of our explanations. And of course we can study the sound waves and other forms of energy involved when they communicate, and those aspects of the physical environment that may be involved. These all have an external reality independent of theory and thus do not have to be created by a special assumption. Their existence can be confirmed by evidence from the senses. They can be and are studied from different points of view. In linguistics they can be studied scientifically from the linguistic or communicative point of view.

We can use the data obtained from people to understand people not indirectly through language but directly from the point of view of how they communicate. The unjustified assumptions of the traditional objects of language could then be given up. The psychological and social reality of grammar fallacies would be avoided. It would be possible to develop explanations of linguistic phenomena of the sort we have been striving for, in terms of people, directly on the basis of the evidence from people, not indirectly through language. Such a linguistics would be a human linguistics rather than a linguistics of language. It would seek a scientific understanding of how people communicate.[2]

Let us consider some possible objections to this alternative proposal.

Perhaps such a course would be open to charges of psychologism. Recall that Bloomfield criticized the earlier linguistics for insisting upon "psychological" interpretation. Statements about language were accompanied "with a paraphrase in terms of mental processes which the speakers are supposed to have undergone. The only evidence for these mental processes is the linguistic process; they add nothing to the discussion, but only obscure it" (1933:17). Bloomfield appears to be combating here the psychological reality of grammar fallacy. But of course the fallacy only follows if one accepts the route through language to the psychological reality. Although Bloomfield did search for psychological foundations for linguistics, he always retained the assumed objects of language, and in his major work he resolutely abandoned any program for achieving a psychological explanation. The inhibitions that were then set up in the discipline discouraged linguists from even thinking about people, and ushered in an era of linguistic Victorianism that is only now coming to an end as an interest in people overcomes an aversion to fallacy. But if we don't assume the objects of language in the first place, we are not confronted with Bloomfield's dilemma of either condoning a fallacy or abandoning the possibility of explanations in terms of people. Without language blocking the way, we are free to move directly from the data obtained from people to theories and proposed explanations in terms of people.

It has been claimed, following Bloomfield and under the influence of behaviorism, that we have no right to guess about the linguistic workings of an inaccessible 'mind', because they are quite simply unobservable. But this was put forth within the context of objections to defining the phoneme as a mental or psychological reality because such definitions would "identify an entity which is inaccessible to scientific methods within the frame of linguistic study" (Twaddell 1935:9), in other words, inaccessible to methods of study through the objects of language. The objection is thus directed at the psychological reality of grammar fallacy, and from this point of view it is well taken. But it would be a mistake or a perverse view of science to jump from this qualified statement to a flat claim that we can't study people, an existing reality, by observing them, while yet maintaining that we can apply some of those observations of people to elucidating the nature of language, a collection of convenient fictions simply introduced by assumption.

Perhaps such a course would lead us toward infinity. Saussure (1916:25;1959:9) had worried that without placing both feet on the ground of language as the integral and concrete object of linguistics we would be confronted with a mass of heterogeneous and unrelated things, and the door would be open to several sciences—psychology, anthropology, normative grammar, philology, etc.—which might claim speech as one of their objects. Recall also that Bloomfield (1933:78) had worried that without a special assumption linguistics would require the near perfection of all branches of science, including, especially, psychology and physiology. He said that the situations which prompt people to utter speech include every object and happening in their universe, requiring for a scientifically accurate definition of meaning a scientifically accurate knowledge of everything in the speakers' world. The actual extent of human knowledge is very small compared to this (1933:139).

The fear is overblown and unfounded. Omniscience is not required. In the first place, when people cooperate by means of sound waves we need not be concerned about a complete scientific knowledge of the things they talk about. We do not need the chemist to tell us everything about NaCl in order to handle *Please pass the salt*. Techniques are available in lexicography for deciding how much material to include. In the second place, the fear may stem precisely from the choice of an approach through language and its philosophical foundation in the theory of knowledge. The methods of grammar are not appropriate for studying the psychological and social aspects of how people communicate, so it was thought that to venture into these domains at all would embroil the linguist in a whole other discipline with completely different concepts, methods, and goals. One would recoil from such a prospect and insist on preserving the autonomy of grammar within its narrow borders even though that meant not being able to confront the communicative relevance of speech events. But if we study people from the point of view of how they communicate, there would be natural interfaces with the various other neighboring disciplines that study people from other points of view. It would become easy to set up convenient disciplinary boundaries and to have fruitful commerce across them. Linguistics would then lose the isolation imposed by grammar, and at the same time it would become more relevant to those adjacent disciplines where linguistic questions arise.

Perhaps such a course would get bogged down in complexities. It is sometimes suggested that we can never achieve a scientific understanding of people because they are too complex. It is true that people are complex, and their communicative abilities and behaviors are among their most complex aspects. This may be one of the reasons that the human sciences are not yet as highly developed as the other sciences. Differences in the complexity of the phenomena involved are perhaps a major reason why science had its first successes in physics, then in chemistry, and later in molecular biology. But science has been able to deal with complexity where it is found in these other sciences. Fear of complexity is no reason not to try a second-alternative approach in linguistics. Linguists have considerable experience already in dealing with complexity in the traditional approach through grammar.

Perhaps such a course could not be carried out because, as is sometimes supposed, you can't do experiments on people for one reason or another, or you can't get scientific evidence about their internal states and ideas. A similar objection regarding the difficulty or impossibility of doing experiments could be raised in the fields of astronomy, human biology, medicine, and elsewhere, but that does not prevent these endeavors from being scientific. Actually, observation and experiment have been extensively used in the other human sciences and even in linguistics. One can obtain experimental evidence about people in several ways. For example, one can observe people engaged in communicative behavior under controlled conditions, videotape what happens, and study it. Alleged difficulties in observation and experiment do not constitute a valid reason for discounting a scientific approach to the phenomena.

This objection sometimes reflects a first-alternative orientation where evidence from observation may not be obtainable. But the issue with which we are concerned is not the place of evidence from the senses in establishing the foundations of such first-domain areas as epistemology, logic, and pure grammar. Rather, the issue facing linguistics is a choice between a first-alternative and a second-alternative approach.

It is sometimes urged against a human science that people are different. Their behavior cannot be predicted. They will do whatever they please. One can never achieve experimental control. This objection has a certain Alice-in-Wonderland quality. Surely we now understand in linguistics that communicative behavior involves constraints. A person cannot in general say whatever he pleases and expect to be understood. Questions of the freedom of the will have been brought up before in linguistics, but this issue is a red herring that would draw our attention away from the contingent nature of prediction everywhere in science. The issue is only whether the study of these constraints will be disciplined by grammar and logic in the first domain or disciplined by science in the second. There is no reason to assume that people are not a part of nature or that they are somehow exempt from the laws of science. It is simply the task of science to find the relevant laws, whatever they may turn out to be.

Perhaps such a course would involve us in giving up too much of what has already been won through the study of language and grammar. This danger will have to be weighed against the advantages of ridding linguistics of what is probably its major source of difficulties and the stimulus for the repeated reworking of grammatical theory in scores or hundreds of attempts. The insights already won would not be lost: they remain recorded in the literature. Valid insights would be available, when needed, to be translated or reworked appropriately into a human-linguistic framework. Since the new framework would cover all the observable phenomena traditionally considered, one would expect that there would be a principle of correspondence roughly relating the two sorts of theories. The carrying over of insights into a new sort of theory would be more difficult than into yet another reworking of grammar, but the results of focusing on a reality would be sounder and more adequate, and thus prove to be more permanent.

On the second alternative, then, linguistics would take up the direct study of people, individually and collectively, from the point of view of how they communicate. Rather than being a linguistics of language disciplined by grammar, it would be a human linguistics disciplined by science. Under this alternative linguistics would not seek to achieve a scientific understanding of language, which we know to be impossible, but instead to achieve a scientific understanding of how people communicate. The goal that linguistics should seek explanations in terms of people is not only compatible with the goal that linguistics be disciplined by science, it is actually the only way that we can have a scientific linguistics.

The second alternative, retaining the goals of being scientific and of seeking explanations in terms of people, and giving up the goal of studying language, has the epistemological and methodological advantages of modern science now only minimally enjoyed by the discipline. In moving from the logical domain to the physical, linguistics would move from a domain where the metaphysics have always been and still are controversial and unsettled into a domain where the metaphysics are relatively settled and have proven over the last several hundred years to be spectacularly successful as a practical guide for the conduct of scientific research in a number of disciplines.

Extending the methods of science even and especially into the foundations of the discipline should yield in time a core body of observationally supported, tested, and tentatively accepted linguistic theory that could withstand attack by any attempted arbitrary promulgation of new and unsupported foundational assumptions. Since the ultimate criteria would be comparisons of the predictions of theory with reality through observation and experiment, theoretical statements would be subject to test by other linguists and could be accepted or rejected on the basis of objective criteria. Factionalism would be reduced. New observations and data could regularly be compared with the growing body of generally accepted theory, and if they call into question some aspects of that theory, the matter could be put to a test. As the body of generally accepted theory grows, the forefront of research would be widened and the cooperative nature of the discipline increased. Results of different investigations would count for more by being relatable to a wider body of accepted theory, which in turn would provide broader and firmer support for primarily observational research.

Linguistics under this alternative would be hooked firmly into the 400-year tradition of modern science and would be able to partake fully of the advantages of the most finely honed and effective system for the advancement of knowledge that is known. Being a true science, it would not be cut off or isolated from the physical and biological sciences, and as a part of science we can expect linguistics to be strengthened by close relations to these other sciences and to be able to cooperate closely with them in pushing back the edges of ignorance and expanding the area understood by science.

The major disadvantages of the second alternative are tactical. Little is known so far about the detailed architecture of a scientifically sound human linguistics. This disadvantage may only be temporary, however, as quite a bit is already known about its foundations. Another disadvantage is that linguistics would appear to be giving up much of what it has won in previous years and centuries. This disadvantage may also be only temporary if it proves feasible to carry over some of these results into the new structure in modified and carefully tested form. Since grammar has been reworked regularly and often anyway, the considerably larger effort to rework these results into a scientifically acceptable theory may not be out of the question, particularly since objective criteria are now available. If the reworking is done well, and carefully validated against the evidence, we may be able to get it right this time and never have to redo linguistic theory again.

WHERE WE STAND

Let us take stock of where matters stand. To continue with business as usual is ruled out because the goals involved are mutually incompatible: The goal of disciplining our studies by grammar is incompatible with the goal of disciplining them by science because the objects of language are not objects of nature given in advance; they are only created by a point of view. The goal of studying language is incompatible with the goal of seeking explanations in terms of people because of the psychological and social reality of grammar fallacies. Language and people exist in different domains altogether. Since a linguistics based on incompatible goals is incoherent, we are driven to choose either the goal of studying language or the goals of disciplining our studies by science and of seeking explanations in terms of people. Of these two coherent alternatives the first, pure grammar, is not appropriate for linguistics because it does not confront the evidence in its domain. It lacks contact with reality, and it does not lead to satisfying explanations. Thus we are driven to the second alternative, a scientific linguistics focused on people, rather than a philosophical linguistics focused on language.

Another way to approach it is in terms of the entities or objects studied. Both the first alternative and business as usual would study the assumed objects of language, while the second alternative would study only people. First there is the ontological argument. Since on the first alternative and in business as usual we are dealing with human language, which presupposes the existence of people anyway, and on the second alternative people are the only entities needed, any assumption of the objects of language would multiply entities beyond necessity and would be rejected by the principle of ontological par-simony (Ockham's razor). But beyond this, and more decisive in ruling for the study of people in the second alternative rather than the study of the objects of language in the first alternative or in business as usual, is the empirical argument. In the test of theory against observation, the existence of people is confirmed by observation by the senses. They can be observed and studied from a linguistic point of view and from nonlinguistic points of view as well. But this test fails with the objects of language. They cannot be observed by the senses or studied from different points of view. They have no existence independent of theory. Thus again we are driven to the second alternative.

But this means giving up the traditional concepts of language and grammar around which the discipline has always been focused. This is a rather sobering prospect.

It is not surprising that linguistics would have to give up firmly held concepts and methods from an ancient philosophically based tradition if it aspires to become a science, for science does not knowingly tolerate unsupported as-sumptions. The more highly developed sciences, when they crystallized out of philosophy, also had to give up preconceptions deeply rooted in prior philosophical thought or long preserved in the folk culture. Recall, for ex-ample, the problems of a geocentric astronomy, the crystalline spheres, the immutability and perfection of the heavens, the prime mover, the earth as a living being, the flat earth with edges, astrology and divination, alchemy, special creation, pneuma or the breath of life, speaking from the heart, vi-talism, spontaneous generation, the luminiferous ether, and many more. These

all represented older assumptions that could not be justified by the evidence
and had to be given up by science, a move that often met with considerable
resistance from entrenched authority and received opinion but won out in the
end. If linguistics opts for science and gives up studying the objects of language because they are only created by a point of view, it will not so much
be giving up its object of study as finally acknowledging its true object of
study, people.

The question immediately arises: Is the second alternative really feasible?
It should be emphasized at this point that the conclusions already reached
regarding the necessity of a second-alternative approach are independent of
how easy or difficult it may be to develop an adequate human linguistics,
and independent of the merits of any particular suggestions as to how this
might be done. These conclusions establish the necessity of exploring and
developing human linguistics if we are not to abandon altogether any attempt
at a coherent approach to the phenomena of interest in the discipline. It
becomes urgent to find out what kind of a body of theory could be developed
for linguistics on the second alternative.

If linguistics gives up the study of language in favor of seeking a scientific
understanding of how people communicate, what would it use as a theoretical
structure in the place of grammar? That is, for the linguistics of language
disciplined by grammar there is a well-known theoretical structure, learned
by every student of linguistics during his normal course of study. Its shape
is largely independent of whether it also includes an attempt to be scientific
or to seek explanations in terms of people. It is the broad picture of language
as a relation between sound and meaning, given by grammar and lexicon,
conceived in terms of levels and components of grammar, involving paradigms
or processes, structures or rules, and allowing a restricted variety of more
detailed constructs that are variously introduced by different schools of grammatical thought. Developed over the centuries and millennia it is the conceptual foundation underlying every form of grammar, and it has contributed
massively to our folk culture. It is so familiar to every linguist that he can
comprehend a new form of grammar in a few weeks of study, or even develop
one himself in a few years. It is the framework on which are hung the par-
ticulars of every new position. It furnishes the point of view or points of view
that create the assumed objects of study in the linguistics of language—the
forms, meanings, words, sentences, and the like that seem so real to us who
are steeped in that ancient and powerful tradition.

If linguistics gives all of this up, what would take its place?

CHAPTER SIX

A Scientific Foundation for Linguistics

For the last century and a half, efforts have been made to develop a scientific approach to linguistics, but at the foundations of the discipline the grammatical tradition with its basically philosophical or first-alternative orientation is still almost always given priority over science. The second alternative involves extending the approach and methods of science into the very core of the discipline and rebuilding linguistics on the scientific tradition rather than on the grammatical tradition. This is relatively straightforward as long as we focus on people rather than on language, and it will be particularly easy to contemplate for those who have some familiarity with the physical and biological sciences. Indeed the greatest difficulty in charting its direction of development has been to set aside and not be misled by familiar concepts from the linguistics of language and entrenched preconceptions from folk theory. What now appears obvious is not at all obvious when viewed through the distortions of this powerful tradition.

The remaining chapters will briefly outline the foundations of a linguistics without language and without grammar, a scientific linguistics focused on people. Such a linguistics proves to be easily within the reach of science. We will want to understand this alternative well enough to judge its feasibility and to support further consideration of the choice we face.

PEOPLE AS OBJECTS OF STUDY

In a study disciplined by science rather than by grammar, all theoretical statements must be supported by evidence from the senses or on the basis of valid reasoning from the results of evidence from the senses. This necessitates not only setting aside the unsupported assumptions of the linguistics of language but also holding in abeyance any possibly interfering preconceptions concerning the nature of thought, ideas, mind, will, consciousness, sensation, perception, and the like, and concepts of culture, institutions, conventions, and the like. Theoretical statements in these areas do not necessarily need to be set aside for other purposes, but should any of these be needed in the foundations of a scientific linguistics, they would have to be carefully and explicitly justified on the basis of evidence. Without such a Galilean stance toward the tradition we have no protection against possible confusions and fallacies originating in that tradition or in our understanding of it. Science starts with official doubt—the suspension of belief or credulity.

Leaving all such preconceptions aside, we begin by taking as our objects of study only real objects, which exist independently of theory and about which we can obtain observational and experimental evidence from different points of view. We will be concerned with a linguistic point of view, that is, a point of view consonant with the observational scope of linguistics outlined in chapter 2.

As suggested earlier, the objects of study in human linguistics are primarily people, individually and collectively. Their existence is well confirmed by observation. They can be observed not only from a linguistic point of view, but from other points of view as well. Unlike the objects of language they do not need to be introduced by a special assumption. They are already there in the real world.

Sound waves are also involved. Bloomfield noted that individuals in a human society cooperate by means of sound waves (1933:28). He gave as an example Jill seeing an apple in a tree, making a noise with her larynx, tongue, and lips, and Jack vaulting the fence and getting the apple for her. Such transactions are easily observable and can even be made the basis of experiments.

Light and other forms of energy must be included, for gestures and facial expressions cannot be ignored, nor the mechanical energy of a tap on a shoulder or the grip of a handshake. These forms of energy can also be observed and measured, although in some cases the techniques of physical analysis may not yet be as well developed as they are for the sound waves of speech and their physical production and reception.

Physical objects and the physical environment sometimes play an important role, such as lanes, fences, apples, and trees, and sometimes objects with marks on them like newspapers, books, and keep-out signs. These are also objects given in advance that can be studied from other points of view.

In sum, then, the objects of study in human linguistics are primarily people, but also the means of energy flow, and sometimes other physical objects and the physical environment. All these are relevant to a scientific study of people from the point of view of how they communicate.

The next question is how to conceive of the task of human linguistics. Recall that the task of the linguistics of language in business as usual is the scientific study of language, which we know to be incoherent. The task of human linguistics is phrased instead as *the scientific study of how people communicate*. This rejects the goal of studying language, but retains the goals of being scientific and of seeking explanations in terms of people.[1] In this statement of the task, *scientific* is understood in the same sense as in the physical and biological science. *People* refers, as in ordinary language, to real flesh and blood people. And *communicate* refers to the scope of phenomena of interest in linguistics as briefly indicated in the beginning of chapter 2. This term does not have a special technical sense here either. It simply points to the initial scope of the questions we are asking.

SYSTEMS IN HUMAN LINGUISTICS

In order to avoid a possible source of confusion, an explicit terminological distinction is maintained in human linguistics between the major objects of theory and the real objects that they are a theory of. Such a distinction is always honored in science, but not often carried explicitly by means of separate terms. The distinction is especially clear when a model or theory of some real object is tested against observations of the real object. Thus a linguistic model or theory of a real person is called a *communicating individual*, sometimes simply an *individual*; and a linguistic model or theory of a group of real people, large or small, along with the communicatively relevant aspects of their environment, is called a *linkage*.

A terminological distinction will not be enforced, however, for nontechnical terms such as *person, people, group,* and so on. Thus the term *person* will sometimes be used for a real-world person, and sometimes for our everyday-language concept of a person. Care will be taken at all times, however, to make clear whether the real object or our concept or theory of that object is being discussed.

The distinction between communicating individuals and concepts of persons can be understood in terms of how much is covered. Communicating individuals are defined in terms of properties that reflect only those aspects of real persons that are relevant to understanding how they communicate. Similarly, linkages are defined in terms of properties that reflect only those aspects of groups of people and the environment that are relevant to how they communicate. Communicating individuals and linkages, therefore, are abstractions. They include only properties of relevance for linguistics, leaving aside any nonlinguistic properties of people that would belong in theories of real people from other points of view. In this way we exclude from direct consideration in the theory that which is irrelevant to the primary concerns of linguistics.

Sometimes it is of interest to consider how a person communicates in a particular group rather than how he communicates in general. For this we define a *participant* as an abstraction of a communicating individual that includes only those linguistic properties relevant for understanding how the person communicates in that group, i.e., relevant in respect to a particular linkage. For example, a participant representing a person communicating in his work group would exclude the many properties of the individual relevant to how he communicates in other groups but not relevant to how he communicates in his work group.

Thus a participant is an abstraction of a communicating individual just as a communicating individual is an abstraction of a concept of a person. Again this excludes from consideration that which is irrelevant for a given purpose.

A participant is a *constituent* of a linkage. Linkages are composed of constituents. Other types of linkage constituents are channels, props, and settings. *Channels* are abstractions representing the physical means by which the sound, light, or other communicative energy is carried. *Props* are abstractions representing any physical objects that may be relevant, such as clocks that tell the time, doors that are knocked on, and signs that are read. *Settings* are abstractions representing relevant aspects of the physical environment, such as living rooms, ticket counters, and conference rooms. These constituents of linkages are also constructs of theory which are distinguished terminologically from the corresponding real objects.

Communicating individuals, linkages, and linkage constituents are treated as *systems* in a way familiar in science. A system is a representation in theory of a given physical object or group of objects. It is separated from its *environment* by arbitrary *boundaries*. Setting up such systems is our first theoretical act. It formalizes our scope of inquiry at the theoretical level by enclosing a limited domain that we think is coherent and reasonably self-contained. If the objects modeled in the system are not entirely isolated and self-contained, in that they are affected by or affect other objects in the surroundings, then we postulate *inputs* and *outputs* representing physical flows of energy such as sound or light that carry these influences across the boundaries. And if the objects modeled are parts of larger objects, then the inputs and outputs represent the influences that cross the boundaries between the objects modeled and the larger objects. This concept of system is quite different from the concept of system found in the linguistics of language following Saussure and others in that it represents a theory or model of a physical reality, as is the case in the physical and biological sciences (Yngve 1985).

Setting up a system in science is justified on the basis that we are free to decide what part of nature we wish to study. The system boundaries formalize that free decision on our part. There may be many ways of setting up a system, with boundaries differently placed. A wise choice in the placement of system boundaries may simplify the ensuing theory and help to provide insight into the phenomena; an unwise choice may complicate the theory and hinder easy understanding.

Communicating individuals and linkages have external and internal boundaries.

The external boundary of a communicating individual usually coincides with the conceptual boundary of the physical organism, but it may include such objects as pencils, eyeglasses, clothing, and other extensions of the person, and it may exclude parts of the body such as fingers used for counting. The external boundary of a linkage represents the boundary of a cohesive group like a customer and clerk, a family around the dinner table, a committee in a meeting room, the citizens of a town, and so on. Here again, the boundaries are arbitrary and set on the basis of convenience for theory in confronting the observed phenomena being studied. Similar considerations hold for the other types of systems.

The internal boundaries are internal to the person or group. Human linguistic theories are not complete theories or models of people; they are only theories of how they communicate. Any scientific theory is limited to certain aspects of some portion of reality. Physics, for example, concentrates on the physical properties of matter, while chemistry concentrates on the chemical properties. A more complete model or theory would be concerned with both. In terms of Bloomfield's Jack and Jill example, human linguistics would introduce two communicating individuals as models of the two persons, and a linkage to model the pair. These would be set up to show how they communicate, but they need not be concerned with modeling why Jill wants the apple or why Jack is willing to get it for her. Such questions could well be relegated to other disciplines. The internal boundaries of our systems, then, are the boundaries within the persons and within the groups that separate the linguistic properties of the persons and groups, the properties of direct concern to linguistics, from the nonlinguistic properties, the properties which are not of direct concern to linguistics.

The units of analysis in human linguistics, then, are not sentences with properties of declarative or interrogative; not words with properties of case, gender, or tense; not phonemes with properties of consonantal or grave; and not features. These would need to be introduced by assumption. They are instead people, individually and collectively, conceived in linguistic theory as communicating individuals and linkages having properties modeling how people communicate. These properties are postulated so as to account for the evidence, and they must be carefully tested against observations by the senses of real people.

Thus the framework of human linguistic theory is basically quite different from the framework of the linguistics of language. Yet inasmuch as it has to account for the same evidence, and more besides, one would expect the two theories to exhibit certain parallels and correspondences. These can be of great help in developing human linguistic theory as long as we take care not to be confused by the psychological and social reality of grammar fallacies, for words, sentences, and the like, or grammars and lexicons, are by no means properties of people.

THE LAW OF COMPONENTIAL PARTITIONING

Since we are laying the foundations of a new theoretical structure, it will be necessary to justify everything with the greatest of care so as to guard against errors at the very beginning that might have unwanted repercussions later. Therefore it is appropriate to ask whether there really is proper justification for defining communicating individuals, participants, and linkages in terms of properties.

The usual initial tactic in the linguistics of language is to introduce speech-sounds, forms, meanings, and other objects of language. Bloomfield, for example, said that the linguist focuses on the speech-signals, and for this he introduced his fundamental assumption of linguistics: "In every speech-community some utterances are alike in form and meaning" (1933:78). Distinctions of "the same" or "different" were to be obtained from the everyday knowledge of the linguist, by trial and error, or from someone who knows the language. Application of a method of sames and differents then led to postulating the properties of these linguistic objects that had been introduced by assumption. Although this tactic gave the methods the look of being empirical and scientific, it did not lead to a coherent linguistic science.

Human linguistics, not accepting any assumptions of the objects of language, departs from the usual sorts of analysis. Bloomfield himself provided an important hint when he noted that "the difference between distinctive and non-distinctive features of sound lies entirely in the habit of the speakers."(1933:77). It is not clear what Bloomfield meant by "habit", and in any event he did not pursue the matter, for he took the distinctions of "the same" and "different" made by speakers and hearers not as evidence about the habits of the speakers and hearers but as evidence about features of speech-sounds in an assumed domain of language.

Human linguistics, on the other hand, takes the distinctions made by speakers and hearers directly for what they are: evidence for properties reflecting aspects of the speakers and hearers themselves that are involved with the production and reception of sound waves and other forms of energy when they communicate. A method of sames and differents is then applicable to working out the properties representing aspects of these real objects. By this straightforward and obvious tactic the need for assuming the objects of language is eliminated and the psychological and social reality of grammar fallacies are avoided.

Let us examine this program in a bit more detail.

We start with an observational fact: different people show communicative differences and the same person shows communicative differences at different times. The same is true for groups. Different groups show communicative differences and the same group shows communicative differences at different times. Perhaps in reality no two people or no two groups are ever exactly alike, and no person or group is ever twice the same, but this does not need to be assumed. All that is needed is the easily verifiable fact that differences are widely observed. It means that the theory will have to confront the possibility of a very large number of systems, all different.

The way in which the theory can confront a very large number of systems, all different, stems from another observational fact: different people show communicative similarities and the same person shows communicative similarities at different times. The same is true for groups of people: different groups show communicative similarities and the same group shows communicative similarities at different times. Again it may well be that any two people will show similarities, and any two groups will show similarities, but this does not need to be assumed either. All that is needed is the easily verifiable fact that similarities are widely observed.

Evidence of communicative similarities and differences of people can be obtained from informant methods, field methods, experimental methods, and other observational methods. By these means data can be obtained on the communicative similarities and differences of different people and of the same person at different times, and of different groups and the same group at different times.

We interpret these observations of similarities and differences as flowing from underlying similarities and differences in the real people and groups themselves. On this basis we postulate properties of the communicating individuals and linkages. The properties are theoretical constructs set up to represent the real similarities and differences and thus to account for the observations of similarities and differences. Some of the properties are relatively permanent. Others are changeable, and it is their changes that account for the observed communicative behavior. Some of the properties parallel direct observation, but many are set up on the basis of indirect evidence. A person may be represented as a communicating individual with properties of having a high voice, or low, or as having a contrast between *caught* and *cot,* or between *pin* and *pen*; or a student in a classroom may be represented as raising his hand. A group may be represented as a linkage with properties of discussing a particular topic, or there may be eye contact between a teacher and a student.

The justification for postulating properties, then, is the observational evidence of communicative similarities and differences of people and groups of people, and the usual presumption of causes found everywhere in science, and indeed in everyday common sense. That is, if we observe similarities and differences of people, the similarities and differences must be caused by underlying similarities and differences in the people themselves, which we model in terms of properties.

On the basis of these considerations, we are justified in proposing an observationally based law, the *law of componential partitioning* (Yngve 1984):

> The communicative aspects of a person, or of a group and the communicatively relevant parts of its environment, can be represented as a communicating individual, or a linkage, in terms of a set of component properties in respect to which different individuals or linkages show partial similarities and differences and in respect to which the same individual or linkage shows partial similarities and differences at different times.

This is the most general law of communicative behavior. It underlies the whole of human linguistics in much the same way as Bloomfield's assumption underlies the whole of the linguistics of language. But rather than being an unjustified special assumption, it is an empirical law supported by the publicly available and reproducible evidence of observed similarities and differences of real objects.

This law reflects the most basic way in which communicating individuals and linkages are structured—in terms of properties. The structuring in terms of properties is of great significance for the conduct of research, for it holds out the hope of reasonably independent studies of single component properties or small sets of properties and their interrelations.

PROPERTIES OF PEOPLE

Human linguistics is not unique in the way it analyzes its subject matter in terms of properties. There are parallels in many other sciences. For example, the chemical properties of elements and compounds in chemistry are theoretical constructs postulated on the basis of observations of similarities and differences in the behavior of different aggregates of real matter in chemical reactions. In classical genetics, constituents of biological organisms (genes) are postulated as theoretical constructs representing certain properties that account for the observations of similarities and differences of real plants and animals, and how the similarities and differences propagate through different generations.

These examples and others that could be cited are strictly parallel to the way in which human linguistics postulates properties of communicating individuals and linkages on the basis of observations of similarities and differences of different people or different groups, and the same person or the same group at different times.

Formalizations in human linguistics are thus based on properties. Two sets of properties are initially defined, a dynamically changing set of properties called *conditional properties* and a more static set of properties called *categorial properties*.

The conditional properties reflect the momentary state or condition of the individual at any instant of time; their changes accompany communicative behavior in regular ways. For example, a person may have the turn in conversation at one moment, and at the next moment not, or at any instant he may be on the spot to answer a question or not, or he may have referred to a particular person rather than to some indefinite person.

The categorial properties represent the categories or dimensions along which these changes take place. For example, there would be categorial properties of being able to have the turn in conversation or not, and of being able to be on the spot to answer a question or not. Categorial properties are relatively unchanging. The categorial property of being able to have the turn in conversation or not will have developed in childhood and remain relatively unchanged throughout life, while the conditional property of now having the turn, and now not having it, will change many times as the person communicates.

It will be seen shortly that there are other types of properties, and that the properties of individuals and linkages are structured in complex ways.

It is worth noting that binary properties of individuals and linkages are completely sufficient in principle for reflecting how persons or groups are the same or different with respect to a battery of observational tests. It is well known that complex tests can be resolved into simpler binary tests, and it is well understood that continuous variables can be characterized to any degree of accuracy by means of binary variables.

If the principle of correspondence with the linguistics of language suggested on p. 41 holds here, most properties can be expected to be naturally binary. However some properties such as phonetic tongue height may seem to require continuous variables. But in this case neither the speaker nor the listener can distinguish phonetically more than a certain number of tongue heights, and a discrete representation would be perfectly satisfactory. In practice, however, it may sometimes be convenient to use nonbinary or even continuous notations in the theory, recognizing that they could be reduced to binary notations.

Another important point is that with only a few properties many different individuals can be distinguished. Although it might require thousands or millions of properties to fully characterize a communicating individual, yet with only 300 binary properties it would be possible to distinguish more than 10^{90} different individuals. If the properties were not uniformly distributed over the individuals, more properties would be required, but in any case it appears that a very large number of different individuals can be distinguished by means of relatively few properties.

Thus we see that the unit of generalization in human linguistics, as in other sciences, is the property. By means of properties we can actually make generalizations even if no two people or no two groups are ever the same or no one person or group is ever the same at different times.

CHAPTER SEVEN

Laws of Communicative Behavior

We have seen how linguistic generalizations can be formulated in terms of properties on the basis of observations of particular persons and particular groups. With these generalizations we will be able to develop specific causal laws of communicative behavior, which should then lead to a proper scientific understanding of how people communicate. In order to move in this direction we will need to expand the foundation already laid in the law of componential partitioning by formulating two additional general laws. These can also be scientifically justified on the basis of easily obtainable evidence.

DYNAMIC CAUSAL STATE THEORIES OF PEOPLE

Let us start by considering the conditional properties of a communicating individual or a linkage. These are the properties that change, with an individual or linkage either having the property or not in a binary representation. A conditional property is the value of the related categorial property. It can be represented as zero or one, for the individual either having the condition or not at any given time. For example, an individual's condition of having the turn in conversation at a certain moment will be represented by a value of one for one of the properties, and not having the turn will be represented by a value of zero.

An individual or linkage will be characterized at any given instant of time by a zero or one for each of the many conditional properties. The total set of zeros and ones representing the conditional properties at any given instant is the *state* of the system at that instant.

Changes in the state of a system take place whenever any one or more of the properties change from zero to one or from one to zero. Since conditional properties are discrete values, any change in value is discontinuous, values intermediate between zero and one being ruled out in a binary representation. When one or more properties change at a given instant, the system is said to have undergone a *transition* at that instant from an *initial state* to a *final state*. The initial state can then be represented as one set of zeros and ones and the final state as a different set of zeros and ones. Transitions occur in sequence.

The final state of one transition becomes the initial state of the next transition. The state does not change between transitions, but remains constant for some interval of time. The intervals of time between transitions may vary.

Some of the conditional properties represent externally observable changes of a person during communicative behavior, such as the movements of the lungs and vocal tract resulting in speech sounds, or the movements of the body seen as gestures and facial expressions. These properties then serve as outputs from the system. Thus the verbal and nonverbal behavior of asking a question would be represented in the theory as the changes of many conditional properties in a carefully controlled time sequence.

There are also many properties that are hidden: They do not directly represent observable characteristics of the person. Such properties are postulated on the basis of indirect evidence from communicative behavior, and sometimes from associated noncommunicative behavior as well. For example, when a person has been asked a question, he is on the spot to provide an answer or some other appropriate response. Being on the spot could be represented by a one value of a hidden property that would only become zero when the person had answered the question or got himself off the spot in some other way. The evidence for the property of being on the spot or not comes from observations of similarities and differences of people related to their observable question-and-answer behavior. As another example, a hostess may ask her guests whether they would prefer coffee or tea. Her subsequent nonlinguistic behavior of bringing each guest the desired beverage is evidence of hidden properties involved with her understanding what they had replied.

What could cause the state of an individual to change? The causes of a transition could only be internal to the individual or external to the individual. Causes in this sense are theoretical entities postulated to reflect the real-world causes of the relevant changes in the person.

The internal causes are to be found among the conditional properties of the initial state of the transition. This initial state set contains conditional properties resulting from earlier transitions; thus they constitute the relevant history of the individual brought forward to the instant before the transition takes place.

The external causes all act across the boundary of the individual.

Some external causes arise in the external environment, reflecting input energies to the person from his surroundings. Examples of these would be the incoming sound waves of speech or the incoming light waves from a smile, a raised eyebrow, or a gesture.

Other external causes arise in properties of the person that are external to the communicating individual and influence the individual across the internal boundary between the individual and the rest of the person. An example would be Jill's decision to ask Jack to get her an apple, which could be represented as a nonlinguistic property of Jill.

The external causes are treated in the same way as the internal causes. Those that are properties of the person external to the individual are already properties, and those that represent the detection of input energies can be treated as causes in the same way as properties.

Thus the causes of any transition are completely contained in the initial state set of properties and the initial set of external causes. A transition, therefore, is characterized or described by these two initial sets, by the final state set of properties, and by the interval of time since the last transition.

We now postulate that the relation between possible sets of causes and possible final sets is mathematically a functional relation: When a transition takes place the final state set is uniquely determined by its causes, which are the initial state set and the set of external causes. This conforms to the ordinary assumption of causality in science that has been so successful in the conduct of scientific research.

Since there are more combinations of possible initial state sets and sets of external causes than there are final state sets, the function is many to one—the same final set may be caused by any one of many different sets of causes.

The interval of time between the previous transition and the current one is the time delay associated with the transition. This time delay is also determined uniquely by the initial sets.

We have arrived at a characterization of an individual or a linkage in terms of a very large list of the possible transitions of the system and a list of the associated time delays. Each transition is characterized by its initial set of causes, its final set of conditional properties, and the time delay.

It should now be pointed out that when an individual or a linkage is characterized in this way, it is being characterized by means of a dynamic causal state theory, a type of theory that is well known in science, going back more than 300 years, and is widely used today in many scientific and engineering disciplines.

However, the theory at this stage is quite intractable. No state set will ever be the same as any other state set if no two individuals are ever the same, or any one individual twice the same. Therefore no one transition will ever be the same as any other transition. And since the number of properties is very large, the number of different state sets is astronomical, as is the number of different possible transitions. Thus as the theory now stands, we do not have any generalizations regarding transitions that could provide specific predictions about communicative behavior that could be tested against the evidence.

What is needed are valid generalizations regarding specific transitions or sets of transitions for particular individuals and linkages. These would constitute specific dynamic causal laws of communicative behavior that would provide predictive power and insight. The way to obtain these is to consider first some further lines of evidence and try to develop further general laws that will reduce the number of possible states and transitions given by the theory.

THE LAW OF SMALL CHANGES

There is considerable observational evidence for the predictability, consistency, and long-term stability of people from the point of view of how they communicate. Relative stability is observed in a person's vocabulary, regional dialect features, and long-term memory for people, objects, and events of communicative significance. People can carry on a coherent conversation, which means that certain of their properties relevant to the conversation remain stable for appropriate lengths of time during the conversation. Stability of properties is also found in the phenomena traditionally analyzed in terms of grammatical or syntactic restrictions between different parts of a sentence. Such evidence for the consistency and predictability of people is widespread and incontrovertible.

In view of this evidence, we are led to a second observationally based general law of communicative behavior, the *law of small changes*:

> Most of the properties of an individual remain stable and unchanged over considerable periods of time; thus only a few properties are changed during each transition.

This important law recognizes that individuals are highly structured in terms of stable groups of properties. Individuals do not suffer extreme fluctuations in their properties. Any large changes must be gradual, the result of the changes of only a few properties at a time. It also appears that properties are graded in terms of their frequency of change. A few may change fairly rapidly, for example the properties at the phonetic and phonological level during ongoing speech. Those that reflect sentence production or understanding would change a bit more slowly. Others reflecting the course of a conversation would change more slowly still. And properties reflecting vocabulary or dialect features would be the slowest to change. Thus there is a possibility of a level structure of properties. At each level there would be properties that change relatively rapidly against a background of more slowly changing properties.

THE PRINCIPLE OF CONTINUITY OF COMPONENT PROPERTIES

The law of small changes leads to the possibility of studying the changes of only one property at a time.

Let us consider a particular conditional component property p_k and what happens to p_k when a transition takes place. With this limitation we will speak of *component transitions*, that is, transitions only from the point of view of what happens to p_k.

Now consider how p_k changes during a component transition. There are only four possibilities. Either p_k changes from zero to one during the component transition or from one to zero, or it does not change, remaining zero or remaining one.

Since according to the law of small changes only a few properties change during each transition, we expect that most of the component transitions are of the sort where p_k does not change. It would thus be a great simplification if while studying p_k we could ignore all the component transitions where p_k does not change. We can do this by introducing a *principle of continuity of component properties*:

A component property will remain the same unless caused to change from time to time by transitions occurring at those times.

This is simply a notational convention by which we agree that when studying a given component property p_k, we will remove from consideration all those transitions where p_k in fact does not change. Since on the law of small changes we expect that p_k does not change during most transitions, the remaining set of component transitions forms only a small subset of the original set of component transitions for p_k, and this brings a great simplification in the theory. Under the principle of continuity, then, when we speak of component transitions we will be speaking only of members of this small subset where p_k does change.

Adopting the principle of continuity of component properties brings the obligation that we try to find and consider all of the component transitions for p_k, for it is assumed that p_k does not change if no corresponding component transition is listed. We hope that the component transitions will be few enough that we will eventually be able to find them all.

The principle of continuity of component properties can be considered as a particularly simple means of formalizing the memory properties of the individual. A property will remain stable unless changed. That is, once the value of a property has been set by a transition, that value will be retained or remembered until it is caused to change again by a transition at some later time.

THE LAW OF RESTRICTED CAUSATION

Let us now look at the component transitions, those transitions where p_k changes. So far there are no restrictions on the causes of component transitions—as far as we now know the causes could include every component property and every external cause. There is evidence, however, that the causes of component transitions are far fewer than this.

We can set up an experiment to elicit the same small segment of communicative behavior from a number of different people and from the same person on multiple occasions. Since this can easily be done, we can conclude that most of the properties where the different people differ and where the same person differs on different occasions are probably irrelevant as causes for the component transitions associated with this small segment of behavior. We can also eliminate as causes for the component transitions all those external causes reflecting irrelevant parts of the surroundings like background noise, different objects in the vicinity, different other people in the group, and so on.

There is also evidence from limitations on the focus of attention. A person concentrating on or attending to a certain topic often does not simulatneously consider other topics, or if he is attending to certain inputs he does not respond to other inputs, as if they were not there.

It is also relevant that it is often rather easy to elicit a given facet of communicative behavior from a person. Because the law of small changes holds, the easy elicitation probably requires the change of only a few properties. However, more permanent cultural factors may also be involved as causes, but the number of these that are directly relevant as causes is also probably small if the facet of behavior elicited is as small as the change of a single property.

Such evidence leads to the third general law, the *law of restricted causation*:

Although the number of component properties is very large, the number involved as causes in the changes of any given component property is small.

This means that when we represent the set of component transitions for any component property we will not have to consider most of the component properties of the individual; only a small number will ever be involved. This law therefore makes possible a considerable further simplification in the theory: component transitions for p_k involve only a small number of properties in their causes.

SPECIFIC DYNAMIC CAUSAL LAWS OF COMMUNICATIVE BEHAVIOR

But much more can be achieved: These three general laws—the law of componential partitioning, the law of small changes, and the law of restricted causation—make possible the development of the specific causal laws of communicative behavior that we have been seeking.

It is a direct implication of the law of restricted causation that in the list of component transitions for p_k most or all of the transitions listed cannot be distinguished from others in the list because they have identical causes. That is, the list contains subsets of identically represented component transitions which come from original transitions only differing from each other elsewhere in their causes.

For each of these subsets of identically represented component transitions we need represent only one. This vastly reduces the number of component transitions represented for p_k.

Furthermore, according to the law of restricted causation only a small number of causes will be involved. This means that there will be only a small number of remaining differently represented component transitions. With a binary representation, 10 causes will allow no more than 1024 different component transitions, 6 causes will allow no more than 64, and 4 causes will allow no more than 16. However it is not yet clear how many causes there will actually turn out to be when we start to analyze data relevant to the changes of specific properties.

The time delays associated with component transitions also need to be adjusted, but this does not drastically alter the conclusions.

Starting with thousands or millions of properties and an astronomical number of transitions, we have found that we can reduce the scope of our consideration to the changes of only one property at a time, and that there will be only a few causes for its component transitions. There is thus the possibility that the differently represented component transitions will be few enough in number that we can find them all. There actually is a chance, then, of achieving a complete representation of the causes for the changes of each component property we study.

It can now be pointed out that:

Each representation of a component transition in this final form is tantamount to a specific dynamic causal law of communicative behavior.

Each such representation says that every time the indicated properties and external causes in an individual reach the values specified, a component transition will take place, changing the property p_k appropriately. Such a representation is a true generalization because there are many ways in which this can happen—the irrelevant properties may take many different sets of values. It has predictive power since it records what will happen under specific repeatable circumstances. It is thus a specific law that can be tested. It is a dynamic law because it deals with the changes of the property p_k. And it is a causal law because it connects the specified change of p_k to its causes.

It turns out that the same considerations hold for linkage properties, and linkages can also be treated in terms of specific causal laws such as these.

THE REPRESENTATION OF CAUSAL LAWS

What remains to be done with these specific dynamic causal laws is purely notational. But notational matters are not unimportant, for they can make a considerable difference in the facility with which research can be carried out and the clarity with which the results can be presented.

Instead of using zero and one as values for the properties in the state set, we can adopt a truth-functional notation in which p_a means that it is true that the property p_a has the value one, and $-p_a$ (not p_a) means that it is not true that p_a has the value one; i.e., it has the value zero.

Suppose we have a dynamic causal law that says that p_k changes to the value zero whenever it is the case that the properties p_a, p_b, and p_c in the state set of the individual take the values of one, zero, and one respectively. Then, since these values must simultaneously hold, we can combine them with the truth-functional *and*, which we write as $\times$.

Using this notation borrowed from logic, and adding the nonlogical notation :: (which we read as *sets*), we can write the causal law as

$$p_a \times -p_b \times p_c :: -p_k$$

which we read as p_a *and not* p_b *and* p_c *sets not* p_k, or in full, *the logic expression "p_a and not p_b and p_c" becoming true sets p_k to the value zero (false)*. We call this a *setting expression*.

Suppose this is the only dynamic causal law that sets p_k to zero. But in general there will be a number of causal laws that are equivalent in that they all set p_k to the same value. For instance, we may have the following causal laws for setting p_k to the value one:

$$-p_a \times -p_b \times p_c :: p_k$$
$$-p_a \times p_b \times p_c :: p_k$$
$$p_a \times p_b \times p_c :: p_k$$

Since these are equivalent causes for the same thing, they can be combined by the logical (inclusive) *or*, which we symbolize as $\lor$. This gives

$$(-p_a \times -p_b \times p_c) \lor (-p_a \times p_b \times p_c) \lor (p_a \times p_b \times p_c) :: p_k$$

For any property p_k there are two equivalence classes of causal laws: one where p_k changes to the value zero and one where it changes to the value one. Thus if the above causal laws cover all the cases, we can express all the changes in p_k by means of the two setting expressions:

$$\begin{cases} p_a \times -p_b \times p_c :: -p_k \\ (-p_a \times -p_b \times p_c) \lor (-p_a \times p_b \times p_c) \lor (p_a \times p_b \times p_c) :: p_k \end{cases}$$

This is called a *setting procedure*.

Other notations are also available for setting procedures, but this notation will be sufficient for carrying the argument forward at this point.[1]

We may need to consider also the time delays in the changes of the property p_k. There are straightforward notational means available to do this. The choice of notation will be influenced strongly by what observation reveals about how the time delays depend on the causes. Since such data are not yet available, we will not consider the matter further at this point.

One of the advantages of borrowing a notation from logic for the causes in setting procedures is that we can make use of the known methods of simplification of logic expressions. In the case at hand, the second setting expression can be simplified, so that the setting procedure can be written

$$\begin{cases} p_a \times -p_b \times p_c :: -p_k \\ (-p_a \times p_c) \lor (p_b \times p_c) :: p_k \end{cases}$$

Another advantage of using the notation of logic is that we can explicitly show by symbolic manipulation whether alternative formulations are equivalent or not. This should help to forestall meaningless arguments.

It is clear that this formulation is completely general. A setting procedure, when correctly formulated on the basis of the evidence, provides a complete and compact representation of the causes for the property to change, and the properties and changes in properties of a communicating individual or linkage can be completely characterized in terms of setting procedures.[2]

In comparing this formulation of linguistic theory with others, whether grammatical or not, it should be kept in mind that this formulation does not rest on any special or a priori assumptions such as Bloomfield's assumption. It does not assume language. It has been proposed in the light of, and justified completely on the basis of, readily available and incontrovertible observational evidence that has been assessed and interpreted with the help of only the most general assumptions of science, which have withstood the test of several centuries of successful application in the physical and biological sciences.

LINGUISTIC PROPERTIES

The introduction of setting procedures introduces into human linguistics what are called *procedural properties*, which stand as a third type of property beside the conditional and categorial properties already discussed.

There is also a fourth type of property. If an individual or a linkage has conditional, categorial, and procedural properties, then the individual or linkage must also have the properties of having such properties. Thus there must also be what we will call *foundational properties*. Foundational properties are required as a foundation on which the other properties are built.

In this picture, then, individuals and linkages are modeled in terms of four types of properties: conditional properties, categorial properties, procedural properties, and foundational properties.

We have seen that the conditional properties or conditions are the changing state properties of the individual or the linkage. Specific configurations of conditional properties selectively trigger or activate any given procedure whenever they match the triggering conditions required for that particular procedure. Then when the procedure executes, it changes one or more of the conditional properties. Conditional properties, when they are changed by the executing of procedures, will stay in their changed state until changed again by the executing of other procedures. Thus they constitute memory properties that record or remember the changing context of situation or changing state of the individual or linkage at every level from phonology to pragmatics—and even, if necessary, the state of the tasks being coordinated by the communicative behavior.

The categorial properties or categories are the dimensions along which the conditional properties vary. They provide the possibilities of change, the categories according to which situations can be represented. Categories are related to conditions as gender is related to feminine, case to dative, or number to plural in the linguistics of language. Categories are not necessarily binary. There may be a number of possible values or conditions, or some may even be represented as continuous variables if that is needed for modeling certain changeable communicative aspects of a person.

The procedural properties consist of procedures, which to some may seem reminiscent of grammar rules. It is important, however, not to confuse them with rules in grammatical theories. Unlike grammar rules, they are not part of a theory of language; they are part of a communicative theory of a person or of a group. They specify the context of conditions under which something will happen, and how what happens then changes this context of conditions. Unlike grammar rules, they are applied or executed on occasion—or better they trigger or activate and execute whenever the stated conditions obtain. They are unordered: All triggering conditions are explicit. And unlike grammar rules, the conditions and changes do not take place in an assumed abstract grammatical or logical domain of a "derivation," or "representation," rather they are part of a dynamic theory that models what takes place in people as they communicate.

The foundational properties contrast with the conditional, categorial, and procedural properties, which together are called *informational properties*. They provide the foundation or support on which the informational properties rest, and constitute the underlying mechanism that makes these properties possible.

Within this framework, specific properties of communicating individuals and linkages are postulated on the basis of observational evidence about specific persons or groups. Since the properties are postulated as parts of theories of real objects, there is the possibility of testing them against further evidence from the real objects. And as we shall see, the properties of communicating individuals and linkages are highly structured, which provides further possibilities for testing postulated interrelations between the various properties.

It is probably worth pointing out that human linguistics does not offer a theory of performance in connection with an assumed competence-performance distinction, since it does not operate with a concept of competence, or indeed of grammar at all. Properties in human linguistics are structured in ways sometimes resembling constructs familiar in grammar, but they are enough different that intuitions about them derived from familiarity with grammatical theories are frequently wrong on account of the psychological reality of grammar fallacy.

Linguistic or communicative behavior is not seen as rule-governed behavior but as lawful behavior. This is just the difference between the logical domain and the physical domain. Our analysis is not reminiscent of the school child laboriously constructing a sentence of Latin by following a rule book, but rather of his practiced, unthinking, and automatic handling of his native language. It has to do with finding the constraints on actual behavior, of accountability to the evidence, not to some ideal or norm. The behavior is seen as being lawful in that it would be exceptionless if we had enough knowledge of contextual factors and of the relevant laws governing their effects. Cases that would be seen as free variation in the linguistics of language would be seen as cases where the relevant constraints are not yet completely known—an invitation to do further research. Similarly, "slips of the tongue" or "mistakes" would eventually have to be accounted for, since we are dealing with a theory of a reality. There is no evidence that people are not subject to the laws of nature. It is up to science to find the laws.

CHAPTER EIGHT

The Linguistic Structure of Properties of People

Let us now move on and see how the theoretical apparatus so far developed can be used in confronting the details of communicative behavior. We will be interested in the ways in which individuals are structured in terms of conditional, categorial, procedural, and foundational properties, and particularly in the influence of context on communicative behavior, which has been difficult to treat under traditional theories.

There are a number of convenient notations and constructions that can be used to represent structures of properties. Several of them will be introduced here without reviewing all of the details of their justification.[1] They can all be set up on the basis of the foundations already given, and on the basis of additional observational evidence attesting to a need for them in representing the observed characteristics of individuals and linkages.

CONTROL PROCEDURES

Let us look again at the example simplified setting procedure of the last chapter:

$$\begin{cases} p_a \times -p_b \times p_c :: -p_k \\ (-p_a \times p_c) \vee (p_b \times p_c) :: p_k \end{cases}$$

This means that whenever the conditional properties constituting the state of the individual take values such that the logic expression on the left in the first line is true, the component property p_k will take the value zero, and when the properties are such that the logic expression on the left in the second line is true, the property p_k will take the value one.

Now suppose that the expressions in parentheses in the second line are found to occur elsewhere, separately or together, in other setting procedures. We could take this as evidence for structure in the individual. The expressions in parentheses might be regarded as representing single properties even though they are made up of the simpler properties p_a, p_b, and p_c that also appear in the first line, and might well also appear elsewhere in other procedures.

We would be justified in postulating two new properties of the individual, p_d and p_e, which have internal structure as given by the expressions in parentheses. These new properties can be formally introduced by means of what are called *control procedures*, which explicitly represent the postulated structures in the individual. In the notation of control procedures we can write

$$-p_a \times p_c : p_d$$

and

$$p_b \times p_c : p_e$$

where we read : as *controls*. Here the control procedure

$$-p_a \times p_c : p_d$$

simply means that whenever it becomes true that p_a has the value zero and p_c has the value one, the property p_d will take the value one with a certain time delay that can also be indicated if necessary. It also means that whenever these properties take other values so that the logic expression on the left becomes not true, then p_d will take the value of not one, i.e., zero.

Now we can substitute the two new properties for the expressions in parentheses and write the example setting procedure in a simplified form as

$$\begin{cases} p_a \times -p_b \times p_c :: -p_k \\ p_d \vee p_e :: p_k \end{cases}$$

The difference between control procedures and setting procedures is that control procedures do not have memory, whereas setting procedures do. Each of the setting expressions in a setting procedure sets the output to the indicated value, and it retains that value even if the input conditions that set it have changed. The output is only set to the other value when the input expression in the other setting expression becomes true. In a control procedure, on the other hand, the output property retains its value only as long as the input expression remains true. If the input expression becomes false, the output property takes the other value. Thus unlike a setting procedure, which requires a separate setting expression to represent the conditions under which the output property takes its separate values, a control procedure is complete in one expression, because if the indicated conditions do not hold, the output takes the other value.

Control procedures can be used in this way to exhibit structural relations between groups of properties and to allow simplification of the logic expressions in setting procedures. They also have other uses in developing more complex constructions of properties.

MULTIVALUED CATEGORIES

It would be convenient if we had a way of representing multivalued categories. Although binary properties are completely adequate in principle, there are cases where multivalued categories would be useful. They can in fact be expected to be as widely useful in human linguistics as they are in the linguistics of language, where there are categories of case with several values for the different cases, and of gender, with sometimes three or more genders.

If F is the name of a category which has several values or conditions, we can represent the several conditions with a dot notation as F.o, F.1, F.2, and so on. Here the category name is written first with the value name following the dot.

Then if we have four input conditions A, B, C, and D, we can represent a four-valued setting procedure involving the category F as follows:

$$\left\{ \begin{array}{l} \text{A :: F.o} \\ \text{B :: F.1} \\ \text{C :: F.2} \\ \text{D :: F.3} \end{array} \right.$$

Here the input conditions could equally well be complex logic expressions, or they could be the output of control procedures containing complex logic expressions.

Of course one could and probably would use appropriate descriptive names in place of A, F, o, 1, and so on. This would be analogous to the descriptive names found in the linguistics of language, where the category of case might have values of nominative, genitive, dative, and accusative. In the present notation one would write case.nominative, case.genitive, and so on.

This notation is also available for binary categories. Thus instead of using the category name only and writing A and − A as the output conditions for a setting procedure, one could use A.1 and A.o. This allows explicit names for both the category (A) and the conditions (o and 1). Separate descriptive names for the category and for the conditions could be used here also if desired.

Whenever multivalued categories are used, they will also enter into the input expressions in setting procedures and control procedures. In this connection, the expression $-S.2$ would specify the condition that the category S does not have the value 2.

THE HIERARCHY OF CATEGORIES AND CONDITIONS

Let us turn now to a matter of considerable importance: the possibility of a hierarchical structure in the categorial and conditional properties.

To take an example, suppose that an individual has a categorial property TURN, which has the value one when the individual has the turn in conversation and the value zero when he does not have the turn in conversation. And suppose there is another property CONV, which has the value one when the individual is in conversation and the value zero when the individual is not in conversation. Now note that these properties are not independent. A person cannot have the turn in conversation if he is not in conversation.

A way of representing this structural fact is to say that the property CONV is actually composed of a set of two properties: CTURN, which will have the value one if the individual is in conversation and has the turn, and CNTURN, which will have the value one if the person is in conversation and does not have the turn.

Then the property of CTURN is simply another more explicit name for the property TURN, and CONV can be recovered by a recoding with a control procedure:

CTURN v CNTURN : CONV

This means that CONV has the value one if either CTURN or CNTURN has the value one (they will never simultaneously have the value one due to their structural interrelation), and CONV will have the value zero if both CTURN and CNTURN have the value zero.

Thus there are four possibilities for the two properties CONVTURN and CNTTURN:

$-$CTURN x $-$CNTURN   not in conversation

CTURN x $-$CNTURN   in conversation and having the turn

$-$CTURN x   CNTURN   in conversation and not having the turn

CTURN x   CNTURN   does not occur

In general, a property may be composed in this way from two or more properties. It will then have the value one if one or more of the properties of the set has the value one, and the value zero if none of the properties in the set has the value one.

This produces a categorial-conditional hierarchy, for a property may be seen to be conditional with respect to a higher level and categorial with respect to a lower level.

In the present example we see that CONV is hierarchically related to CTURN and CNTURN. At one level we can say that the individual is either in conversation or not, depending on whether CONV has the value one or zero. At a lower level we can say that a person in conversation either has the turn or not, depending on whether CTURN has the value one or zero.

Or, taking both levels into account, we can say that the property CONV is made up of two properties such that there are three mutually exclusive values for CONV: not in conversation, in conversation and having the turn, and in conversation and not having the turn. In this view CTURN is conditional in nature with respect to the higher level in that it can be viewed as one of the values of CONV, and it is categorial in nature with respect to the lower level in that it has two values, one and zero, for having the turn or not at any given moment.

These several facilities already provide a great deal of flexibility for representing the structures found in the categorial and conditional properties of individuals and linkages. Other facilities can be introduced as needed.

THE USE OF FEEDBACK

Human linguistics is a dynamic theory. When a procedure executes, a dynamic process takes place in time that changes the conditional properties. An examination of the structure of procedural properties, then, is also an examination of how the temporal course of communicative behavior is controlled.

As an exercise in the structure of procedures let us consider what would happen if the output property of a procedure were connected back to the input. There would be a time delay, of course, for the execution of a procedure always involves a time delay, a period of time starting when the causal expression on the left becomes true and ending when the output property changes.

Consider the following setting procedure:

$$\begin{cases} trigger :: out \\ out :: -out, d \end{cases}$$

Here we will assume that the input property *trigger* becomes one for a short period of time and then returns to zero. Its becoming one sets the setting procedure so that the output category *out* takes the value one. Note that *out* is connected back as an input condition in the setting expression that changes *out* back to the value zero. But *out* changes to zero only after a specified delay time *d* that is indicated in a standard way after the comma. Therefore, when the property *trigger* becomes one for a short period of time, the setting procedure is triggered, and *out* becomes one for a specified interval of time *d*. We can say that we have generated a *pulse* of length *d* on the output category *out*. This is our first use of the principle of feedback, which is of considerable importance in human linguistics. By means of delays, with and without feedback, the temporal course of communicative events can be controlled.

EXPECTATION PROCEDURES

It is often the case that two or more setting procedures and control procedures operate together in a coordinated way. When this is the case, it is convenient to consider the several cooperating procedures as one complex procedure or construction.

As an example, consider the following complex procedure made up of one setting procedure and one control procedure:

$$\begin{cases} \text{trigger :: expectation} \\ \text{event :: } -\text{expectation, d} \end{cases}$$
$$\text{event x expectation : next}$$

Assume again that the input property *trigger* becomes one for a short period of time. This sets the output category *expectation* to one, and it will remain one until the input category *event* becomes one, setting it back to zero after a specified delay time *d*. Then in the control procedure, *event* and *expectation* simultaneously having the value one controls the output category *next*, which will take the value one only during the time when *event* is still one and *expectation* has not yet returned to zero. (Here we ignore the delay in the control procedure, which we will assume is short compared to *d*.)

We can interpret this as follows: The short trigger pulse *trigger* sets up an expectation that a certain event will occur (that *event* will become one), and this expectation will be remembered until the event does occur, at which time the expectation will be canceled (*expectation* becomes zero) and a pulse will be sent out on the category *next* to trigger the next procedure.

This is a simple example of what is called an *expectation procedure*. It is constructed of one setting procedure and one control procedure. Expectation procedures are widely useful in human linguistics. By means of the *expectation* output, which is one during the time that the event is expected, the system effectively "knows" what it is expecting, and its behavior in the interim can be controlled appropriately. For example, the *expectation* output can be connected to control procedures so as to interpret a potentially ambiguous change in properties as an occurrence of the expected event rather than as what it might be on other occasions. This is one of the ways in which we can handle the influence of context on communicative behavior.

TASK PROCEDURES AND THE HIERARCHY OF TASKS

An important use for an expectation procedure is to implement what is called a *task procedure*, which is a procedure for controlling the execution of a task. Suppose a student executes the task of raising his hand to seek recognition in the classroom. We can make a task procedure for this out of an expectation procedure by relabeling the *trigger* input as *raise* and connecting it also to the mechanism for starting to raise the hand, so that the same short pulse will both set the expectation of the hand being raised and start the activity of raising the hand. Then we can relabel the *expectation* output as *task-active*, or *hand-being-raised*. The expected event, which is the completion of raising the hand, could be signaled by a pulse from a hand-up detector. So we can relabel the *event* input as *hand-up*.

When this task procedure is triggered as the task of raising the hand is started, it sets up an expectation of the completion of that task by a *task-active* or *hand-being-raised* category taking the value of one, and then when the hand is up, the expectation is canceled and the task procedure sends a *next* pulse on to initiate the next step in the communicative behavior.

Note that a task procedure for raising the hand may be specialized for gaining recognition in the classroom. In this case, when the task is completed an expectation for being called on would be set up. But the hand may be raised for other purposes as well, such as reaching for a high book in the bookcase. That task would be controlled by a different specialized task procedure, the completion of which would set up a task of grasping the book as the next activity, rather than an expectation of being called on. By this means the different purposes for the same act would be controlled by separate task procedures, and therefore would not be confused. Thus we see that task procedures do control tasks by placing them sequentially within larger tasks such as answering a teacher's question or looking up an answer in a book.

Now it should already be clear that two or more task procedures can be chained together by sending the *next* output pulse from one procedure to the *trigger* input of the next procedure. Then the task procedures would be executed in temporal sequence. These sequential task procedures could control the sequential steps required in carrying out a complex task.

In this case, we could have an overall higher-level task procedure which would control this string of tasks. It would be set when they start and expect their completion. In this way we can build a task hierarchy with a number of levels of tasks and subtasks. This facility in human linguistics of representing a task hierarchy is very important for dealing with the hierarchical organization of communicative behavior in ways reminiscent of phrase structure in the linguistics of language.

SELECTION PROCEDURES

Another type of procedure important for the control of complex communicative behavior is the *selection procedure*. A selection procedure allows for a choice among several courses of action depending on how the conditional properties are set, thus implementing contextual dependencies of communicative behavior.

Suppose we have a case where one of four different task procedures should be selectively triggered, depending on various combinations of the values of three properties, a, b, and c. Let t be the initial trigger input to the selection procedure, and let the four outputs from the selection procedure be $t1$, $t2$, $t3$, and $t4$. These would be connected as trigger inputs to the four task procedures to be controlled. Given the required combinations of values for a, b, and c, the appropriate selection procedure can be assembled very simply from four control procedures as in the following example:

$$t \times \quad a \times \; -b \times \; -c : t1$$
$$t \times \; -a \times \; -b \times \quad c : t2$$
$$t \times \quad a \times \quad b \times \; -c : t3$$
$$t \times \quad a \times \; -b \times \quad c : t4$$

In this example an input pulse on t will cause a pulse to appear on one of the four outputs, $t1$, $t2$, $t3$, or $t4$, only if the control properties a, b, and c have the appropriate values as indicated.

THE LINGUISTIC COORDINATION OF NONLINGUISTIC TASKS

With these facilities and others that can be constructed straightforwardly out of the available elements, we would seem to have all that is needed for handling the communicative phenomena usually associated with syntax in the linguistics of language.

Furthermore, since the significance of communicative behavior is that by its means people interact and cooperate in groups and societies, linguistic or communicative tasks can be seen as subtasks of higher-level cooperative or interactive tasks such as obtaining food, being helpful (or combative), and the like. For example, within the scope of Jill's nonlinguistic task of getting an apple with Jack's help, the details of the communicative subtask of enlisting his aid are rather narrowly constrained in ways that are of great interest in linguistics. Human linguistics concentrates on the lower-level communicative tasks and only moves up the hierarchy of tasks as far as it needs to for its own purposes. It does not need to provide a theory of or to model nonlinguistic phenomena in such areas as motivation, ethics, higher-level task organization, decision making, or free will.

But at the same time we do not need to close our eyes to relevant evidence from adjacent disciplines or from our prior knowledge of the nonlinguistic tasks that are being coordinated. Jack's behavior in getting the apple for Jill and Jill's behavior in accepting it are relevant data for the linguist even though he does not see it as his business to provide a theory of that behavior or to model it. In fact, a powerful research technique in human linguistics is the careful observation of similarities and differences of communicative behavior and the correlated nonlinguistic behavior when certain aspects of the coordinated tasks are kept constant or systematically varied. By these means we can establish the linguistic distinctions that are being made.

Thus in human linguistics there are two categories of data: observations of linguistic behavior that we wish our models to explain and predict, and related nonlinguistic observations that we do not wish our models to explain or predict, but that we can use as valuable evidence in establishing or testing our theories. In this respect human linguistics resembles the physical and biological sciences, but differs from the usual program of the linguistics of language where the set of observations used as evidence, say a corpus of utterances and judgments of grammaticality, is identical with the set of observations to be explained. This difference reflects the unity and interconnectedness of science and the relevance of human linguistics to its neighboring disciplines, and contrasts with the autonomy and comparative isolation of grammar from other disciplines noticed in chapter 5.

THE HIERARCHY OF LEVELS OF MODELING

There is a third hierarchy in addition to the categorial-conditional hierarchy and the task hierarchy. We have constructed complex procedures out of simpler ones, and we could continue the process, building still other, more-complex procedures out of the complex procedures. This hierarchy is a foundational-informational hierarchy. From this point of view, setting procedures and control procedures are foundational with respect to the expectation procedures that are built on them. At each level there are lower-level constructions in the hierarchy that serve as the foundational properties supporting the informational properties (the conditional, categorial, and procedural properties) that are built on them. This possibility is very important because it allows certain natural simplifications in representing the structures of individuals and linkages.

How about moving down in the other direction? Can we find levels in the foundational-informational hierarchy below that of the setting procedures on which our constructions have been based? It is in fact possible to build up setting procedures completely out of control procedures. This can be done by connecting control procedures together with feedback in what is called a flip-flop connection in computer science. This shows that the principle of continuity of component properties on which the construction of setting procedures rests is, as we thought, simply a convenient notational convention.

At any given level of analysis the foundational properties are considered as unanalyzed but logically required to support the properties that are constructed on them. Thus they can be considered as lying below the limit of verisimilitude of the model at the given level of analysis, the level below which the model no longer attempts to represent the object being modeled. If one were to analyze the foundational properties themselves, they would again be analyzed as informational properties, and again there would be a lower limit, a limit of verisimilitude below which there would be a new lower-level set of foundational properties. At the bottom of this hierarchy in the theory of the communicating individual lies the disciplinary boundary between linguistics and physiology.

CONTEXT AND THE DOMAIN OF CONTROL

A dynamic state system is appropriate for the individual because it allows us to take into account the continually changing context of situation for the individual as it affects communicative behavior and is in turn affected by communicative behavior. The context of situation is modeled in the state properties of the individual (the conditional properties) as they change from moment to moment. What an individual says or does communicatively at any moment depends not only on his repertory of categorial and procedural properties but also on his condition or state at that moment. What an individual understands of the communicative behavior of others depends not only on the input energy of the sounds heard and his receptive repertory, but also on his state at the moment of reception. When certain conditions in the individual obtain, certain things happen. It is for scientific research to find out what the conditions are, how they are structured, and how they help to control the dynamic changes in the individual that constitute communicative behavior.

Recall that according to the law of small changes, only a few properties change at any given moment. And according to the law of restricted causation, the number of properties entering as causes for these changes are again few. These properties which are potentially causal can be understood as constituting the central part of what is called the *domain of control*. Then there are other properties that are nearly ready to be changed, and again there is a limited set of properties figuring causally in possible changes of these other properties.

These can be understood as being further from the center of the domain of control. The domain of control is the human-linguistic analog of the focus of attention, and like the focus of attention it can shift from moment to moment as different sets of properties stand ready to be triggered.

Our research, then, will be centrally concerned with analyzing properties in and near the domain of control. What would we expect to find there? That question in effect asks us to identify all of the conditional properties that figure causally in the communicative behavior we are examining. The causes may be of many sorts, for we understand that the constraints of context encompass all the communicative phenomena that in the linguistics of language would be studied in phonetics, phonology, morphology, syntax, semantics, and pragmatics—and more besides—indeed all of the constraints that operate causally when people communicate. And all of these constraints operate simultaneously. They are unified in the conditional properties, for many different sorts of constraints may operate as conditions in the causal expression for triggering any given procedure.

Now consider what happens when some procedures are triggered. The domain of control of necessity shifts, because new conditions now obtain and different procedures will stand ready or nearly ready to be triggered. In this way we can see how communicative behavior changes the context and affects the understanding of the communicative behavior that follows.

Thus in human linguistics we have an appropriate and ready means for handling contextual dependence of all sorts. This includes the treatment of so-called shifters and indexical expressions, contextually relative referring, tense and time reference, phenomena seen as ellipsis, and phenomena previously treated under pragmatics and presuppositions. It is a characteristic of human linguistics that it provides the means for integrating these many sorts of constraints. And it is a characteristic of the linguistics of language that its traditional theoretical structure lacks any good mechanism for handling contextual factors. Such a mechanism was not introduced into sign theory by the ancients, who focused more on the requirements of logic and the theory of knowledge than on the scientific understanding of how people communicate. Thus they placed the study of speech in the logical rather than the physical domain, where it has remained for two millennia in philosophy and in normative grammar.

THE PRINCIPLE OF EQUIVALENT COMPONENTIAL HISTORIES

The view of causes in human linguistics, then, is that of immediate causes. The causes of a transition are represented in the conditional properties, and it is the current values of the conditional properties that are causally related to whether a certain procedure is executed or not. However, many of the causally relevant conditional properties will have acquired their current values in times past.

This fact has certain implications when considering the temporal antecedents for any given facet of communicative behavior. For a given procedure to be triggered, a logic expression must become true. In general, this could have happened in any one of a number of different ways. For each of the conditions required for triggering, there may be many ways in which that property might have been set to the current value at some earlier time, depending on the particular history of that individual. Further, different properties in the expression might be the last to change. Also, if the logic expression were a disjunction, there would be different ways in which it could become true, depending on which disjunct became true. Thus there are in general many possible histories of the individual that could have led up to the triggering of a given procedure. We can summarize this insight in the *principle of equivalent componential histories*:

A component property or group of properties represents in a compact fashion any one of all those different possible histories or different sets of relevant past events that would influence current communicative behavior in a certain way.

This principle is completely implied by our earlier considerations. Indeed, it is a well-known principle in other formalizations of state theories. It is one of the most important advantages of state theories, for it allows a considerable simplification. In our case it means that we do not have to know the complete details of the history of an individual in order to predict one facet of his behavior. We do not have to be omnipotent in order to make predictions in linguistics. All we have to know is the relevant aspects of the current state of the individual. That state could have been arrived at in any one of a number of different ways. That means that the doubts sometimes expressed about the possibility of a causal linguistic theory are not as well founded as has sometimes been feared.

CHAPTER NINE

The Linguistic Structure
of Communities

One of the incoherences associated with the psychological and social reality of grammar fallacies is the facile assumption that language in the individual is the same as language in the community, and that the identical theory will do for both. But it is quite clear on the basis of observation by the senses that a person is not the same as a group. In human linguistics it is possible to embody these differences in the different but related theories of communicating individuals and linkages, and then study the important and fascinating questions of how the person is related to the group and how the group is related to the people that make it up.

GROUPS AS SYSTEMS

Any set of communicating individuals could be characterized simply in terms of the properties they have in common. We could study the speech of people in a geographic area in terms of a set of individuals, and analyze their similarities and differences in a way resembling standard dialect surveys. Here it would be of interest to know which dialect features, described in terms of properties of the individuals, were common throughout the region, which features varied, and how they varied geographically, socially, and along other dimensions. Historical change could also be treated in this manner. There would be certain advantages in doing this, for our descriptions would be anchored in the people themselves and their similarities and differences, rather than in language. It has been difficult to treat variation using the concepts of language and grammar, which were developed for describing an ideal of perfection, and thus tended to imply uniformity when applied to a community.

But treating a community simply in terms of the distributions of common properties of the individuals would not be sufficiently revealing. A community is more than a set of individuals; it embodies structure reflecting the communicative interactions between the individuals in the community. Taking this structure into account would seem to be necessary if we are to understand more clearly how people communicate. Human linguistics allows us to take this structure into account. We can analyze the structures of groups and communities in terms of systems by means of linkage theory.

Linkages are characterized by properties, as are individuals, but linkage properties and individual properties are different, being related to different sorts of physical objects—to groups of people rather than to single persons. However linkages and individuals, though different, are similarly constituted and structured: They are both analyzed in terms of conditional, categorial, procedural, and foundational properties, and the same general laws hold for linkages as for individuals—the law of componential partitioning, the law of small changes, and the law of restricted causation. This allows a certain symmetry in the theory.

Linkage properties are understood as properties of the linkage as a whole. If two people are in conversation, their joint activity can be represented in terms of linkage properties. If they are talking past each other because there is a mutual misunderstanding, the misunderstanding would be represented in terms of linkage properties, for no person can talk past each other by himself. When the members of a group have agreed on a topic of conversation, the agreement on the topic and the topic itself would be represented in terms of linkage conditional properties, and the coming to agreement would be represented in terms of the executing of linkage procedures. When Jill asks Jack to get an apple for her, the joint communicative activity leading up to Jack getting the apple would be represented as the executing of linkage procedures.

A dynamic state system is appropriate for the analysis of groups because it allows the modeling of such changing group properties as agreeing, disagreeing, bargaining, negotiating a topic of conversation, considering an issue, reaching a consensus, and the like. The standard case in human linguistics is a linkage in which communicating individuals that are similar in some of their properties but different in other properties are communicating with each other.

Recall that a linkage as a system is composed of any number of constituents. These may be communicating individuals as participants, a channel or channels to carry the energy of the sound waves and any other form of energy involved, and possibly props and settings to represent the communicatively relevant aspects of objects and the physical environment. A linkage, then, can be characterized as *large* or *small* in terms of the number of constituents it is made up of. It may contain any number of constituents, from only a few to many millions.

Since a linkage represents an object of aggregation that can be set up and dissolved, it can also be delimited in terms of its temporal boundaries. Thus a linkage can also be characterized as *brief* or *long lasting*. If two people meet on the street and greet each other, we could analyze what happens in terms of a brief linkage. A linkage covering the extent of a friendship would be longer lasting.

Linkages are also characterized as *broad* or *narrow*. A broad linkage involves many properties, as would be the case in a close-knit family. A narrow linkage involves comparatively few properties, as between a housewife and the grocery-store clerk. People in a broad linkage would be said to be well acquainted, having much in common; people in a narrow linkage would be casual acquaintances.

In addition, we recognize analyses in terms of either *focused* or *complete* linkages. A focused linkage analysis of a family might consider only one facet of their communicative behavior, such as what names or nicknames they use for each other. A complete linkage analysis would be concerned with the total communicative behavior in the family.

THE RELATION OF INDIVIDUAL AND GROUP

A communicating individual has been defined as an abstraction of a person that includes just those properties required to understand how he communicates, and a participant has been defined as an abstraction of a communicating individual that includes just those properties required to understand how he communicates in a particular linkage. The properties of a participant, therefore, form a subset of the properties of the communicating individual, just as the properties of the communicating individual form a subset of the properties of the person. The properties of both the communicating individual and the participant are set up and justified on the basis of observed similarities and differences between this person and others and between this person and himself at different times. The properties of a participant, therefore, are relative to a person. Except for their selection, they are not relative to a group. They answer to what the person is doing in his own terms when he is participating in the group.

In terms of the group, however, different people may do the same thing in different ways. For example, a husband and wife in a clothing store may have selected a particular dress from several they like. Either the husband or the wife might go to the clerk and close the sale by saying, "We'll take the blue one." These would be equivalent, for in either case the clerk would write up the order for the selected dress, and in this sense the husband and the wife would be doing the same thing. But their participant properties might be quite different. The husband may use "blue" as selecting one from fifteen or twenty colors, whereas the wife may use "blue" as selecting one from twenty or thirty colors. Everybody is different. It would be unusual if two persons always did the same things in exactly the same way.

So we also want to be able to say that although they are doing it differently, still they are doing the same thing from the point of view of the group. For this we use the concept of a *role part*. A role part is a functional part of a linkage, and its properties are relative to the linkage that it is a part of, rather than to a communicating individual. Thus role-part properties are set up and justified on the basis of observed similarities and differences between different groups and between the same group and itself at different times, rather than between different persons and between the same person and himself at different times as is the case with participants. The relation of participant to role-part is that of form to function. A participant, as a constituent or formal part of a linkage, fills a role part as a functional part of the linkage.

In the example, the linkages are similar in that each has a customer as a role part, but they are different in that one of the linkages has the husband and the other the wife as a participant. In terms of role-part properties, we are able to say that the husband and wife are doing the same thing when they say to the clerk, "We'll take the blue one," for it fills the same function by making the same selection in a customer-clerk linkage—closing the sale— and thus it affects the linkage properties in the same way.

Since the constituents of a linkage include not only participants but channels, props, and settings as well, it is appropriate to define other functional parts of a linkage. These are called *channel parts*, *prop parts*, and *setting parts*. The obvious analogies hold.

A linkage is more than the sum of its parts. The organization or *arrangement* of the parts is also important. As an example, consider a linkage between a concertgoer and a ticket taker as participants, the concert-hall entrance as a setting, and the ticket as a prop. The communicative interaction when the concertgoer presents his ticket and enters the concert hall involves the physical arrangement of both participants with respect to the setting, and the prop with respect to the two participants. As another example, consider a teacher standing in front of a class as one arrangement. Then if a student is to give a report, the student may take the place of the teacher in front of the class in a different arrangement. The communicative phenomena taking place involve not only the teacher and students as participants, but also their arrangement in the classroom as a setting.

We see, then, that the properties of the various functional parts of a linkage—the role parts, channel parts, prop parts, and setting parts—are all set up on the basis of the same evidence used to set up linkage properties, namely, observed similarities and differences of different groups and of the same group at different times. The evidence is just interpreted differently— in terms of linkage properties in one case and in terms of the properties of the functional parts of the linkage and their arrangement in the other case.

We can conclude that a linkage can be described alternatively in terms of linkage properties or in terms of the properties of its role parts and other functional parts, and their arrangement. The two descriptions are of the same thing, a communicatively coherent group, but they are at different levels of analysis.

GENERALIZING OVER GROUPS

Although we suspect that every linkage is different from every other linkage, there are often similarities between linkages that go beyond single linkage properties. Thus there is a possibility for further generalizations.

Suppose we are studying the members of a family from the point of view of what names or nicknames they call each other. We could set up brief focused linkages dealing with situations of direct address between family members. Each instance of one family member directly addressing another would count as a separate brief focused linkage. If the focused linkages were sufficiently limited in scope, there would be cases where a number of focused linkages were identical in their categorial, procedural, and foundational properties, since the differences between the corresponding complete linkages would have been removed from consideration when we focused narrowly on the phenomena of interest. For example, most of the linkages where a member of the family is addressing the youngest son might be identical in involving him being called "Tommy," while the other aspects that show differences would have been set aside.

In cases like this, where two or more focused linkages are identical in their categorial, procedural, and foundational properties, these properties define a *linkage type*. A linkage type is not a linkage, since it does not include the conditional properties, which, being changeable, make any linkage different at different times, nor does it include specified temporal boundaries. It does, however, characterize each of the similar focused linkages in terms of the static properties they hold in common, and these focused linkages will all operate the same dynamically. Thus a linkage type is a generalization over focused linkages that have identical static properties.

For each linkage type we can also define appropriate *role types*, *channel types*, *prop types*, and *setting types*. These are defined in an analogous fashion in terms of the identical categorial, procedural, and foundational properties of the role parts, channel parts, prop parts, and setting parts that are the constituents of the focused linkages of the linkage type. For example, one of the role types would be an appropriate generalization over the role parts representing any family member addressing the youngest son as "Tommy."

INTERACTIONS BETWEEN GROUPS

When studying several people interacting with each other communicatively, it may be worthwhile to consider the phenomena not in terms of one overall linkage, but instead in terms of two or more linkages interacting with each other.

Linkages that interact with each other are said to be *coupled*. When the coupling between two linkages does not involve any third linkage, we say that the two linkages are *directly coupled*. Thus a focused linkage with a man and his employer as participants might be directly coupled to a focused linkage with the man and his wife as participants, even though the employer and the wife may never have met. For example, the employer may suggest to the man that he invite his wife to an office party that is being planned.

In this example the focused linkages are coupled through an individual. The man is a participant in both linkages—he is the employee in one linkage and the husband in the other. And since the linkages are coupled, these two participants in different focused linkages must have some properties in common that account for the coupling. The properties that they have in common approximate what is called the *contact* in the individual between the two linkages. We can say that the two linkages are coupled through their contact in the man. Although the properties in the contact between these two participants in different linkages are identical, being subsets of the properties of the same individual, it must be remembered that the properties of the corresponding role parts in the two linkages will be different, being structured relative to different linkages.

We can distinguish several structural types of direct coupling between linkages.

One type of direct coupling is the messenger type. For example, a skilled negotiator may conduct sensitive negotiations between two countries by acting as a messenger. The messenger moves back and forth between two linkages, being a participant in each, with the linkages being coupled through contact in these two participants in the same individual.

Another type of direct coupling between linkages is the dinner-table type. Consider the case of two friends of long standing who are dining with each other and their spouses. There would be two long-lasting husband-wife linkages and a linkage for the two friends. There would also be a brief linkage of the four of them around the dinner table. What goes on communicatively might best be described in terms of these four linkages and the interactions between them, which are of the directly coupled type through contact in the various participants in the several linkages.

An interesting type of direct coupling is the linkage-creating type. When a person brings one of his friends up and introduces her to another of his friends, and then excuses himself, leaving the two to talk, a linkage has been created between the person's two friends. Here the new linkage is created by contact in the participants in the two initial linkages and in the new linkage across its initial boundary.

A frequent type of direct coupling is the broadcast type of coupling between linkages. A lecturer is a participant in a separate linkage with each member of the audience. Each of these linkages is directly coupled to all the others through contact in the lecturer. There may, of course, be other linkages between different members of the audience, but not necessarily. The result of the contact is commonality of properties in the members of the audience, all having heard the same lecture.

Linkages can also be directly coupled through contact in props, channels, and settings. For example, a family expecting guests in the evening may leave the porch light on to mark the house for the guests. As the guests come up the street looking for the house, the linkage of family and porch light would be coupled to the linkage of porch light and guests through contact in the porch light as a prop.

Writing can be analyzed as a prop. The writer would be a participant and what he is writing would be a prop in one linkage, and the reader would be a participant and the writing a prop in another linkage, with contact between the two linkages in the props. The properties of the props in the contact would be the same in each prop if the reader reads the original, but the prop parts in these two linkages would be different, being relative to different linkages. In this way we can account for misinterpretations on the part of the reader. We can handle in a similar manner other signs, such as cairns of stones, tracks in the snow, and the phenomena of nature.

Alternatively, writing can be analyzed as a channel—a constituent of a linkage standing between the writer and the reader as participants. Here there would be delay in the channel, and the reader may not even be contemporaneous with the writer. The telephone and other electronic means of communication are important in modern culture and do not normally involve much delay. They can easily be analyzed as channels.

Another way in which linkages can be directly coupled is through contact in an arrangement. In a doctor's office with several examining rooms, the linkage between the patients and the nurse is coupled to the linkage between the patients and the doctor through an arrangement of the participants when the nurse ushers the patients into the examining rooms in a certain order so that the doctor will know who is next. Furthermore, she may place each patient's chart on the desk in the examining room so that the doctor will know which patient is waiting in the examining room by the arrangement of this prop.

THE STRUCTURE OF COMMUNITIES

When linkages interact only through one or more other linkages, they are said to be *indirectly coupled* through a chain of directly coupled linkages.

The employer's wife may ask her husband to ask several employees to ask their wives to a party that she is planning. Here the first husband-wife linkage is indirectly coupled through the employer-employee linkage to the second husband-wife linkage.

Chains of directly coupled linkages can also provide the indirect coupling characteristic of the spread of rumors. A rumor can change in two ways. It can change in each linkage because the properties of the participants are relative to different individuals, who may have different understandings. And it can change in each individual in the contact between linkages, for the properties of the role parts are relative to different linkages, allowing for the possibility of paraphrase rather than verbatim repetition.

One way, then, in which the structure of a community can be understood is in terms of the direct and indirect coupling of linkages. Each individual is a participant in many linkages. Some of these will be directly coupled to others, and some will be indirectly coupled to still others. An individual may participate in linkages involving other members of his family, neighbors, friends, and acquaintances. He may participate in linkages with sales and service people, people in his school or place of employment, in government and political organizations, and with other members of a religious organization, lodge, union, or club. He may also participate in linkages with newscasters and public figures through radio and television, and with writers and reporters through his reading of newspapers, magazines, and books. In short, for most people there is a very large circle of others that he participates with in linkages. And these linkages are potentially directly and indirectly coupled to still other linkages in the community. The individual may be linked in this way through word of mouth, and especially through the media, to virtually everyone else in the community.

The picture is that of a complex network with individuals at the nodes. Each individual participates in many linkages with many other individuals. Some of these linkages are directly coupled to each other through contact in his being a participant in each. Some are directly coupled through other individuals to other linkages, and some are indirectly coupled to still other linkages reaching to still other individuals in the community. This network would extend throughout the community, with probably no individual or part of the community completely isolated communicatively from the rest. For some sorts of communicative phenomena, this picture of a community may be especially revealing, but for other phenomena its extreme complexity would be a disadvantage.

At the other extreme one could treat the community simply as a single very large linkage covering the whole community. Some structure could be handled through concepts of the arrangement of the participants, and through statements about the arrangement of properties and changes in the arrangement of properties as news and information flow through the community. This would eliminate the extreme complexity of the network analysis, but at the expense of not allowing for the handling of important elements of structure.

Fortunately there is another possibility. An analysis is possible in which people can communicate with groups, and groups can communicate with other groups. For example, a person may communicate with an organization such as a unit of government, a financial institution, or a utility company, and the unit of government may communicate with the utility company. This possibility is completely implied by the theory as it stands, because linkages as well as individuals are defined in terms of conditional, categorial, procedural, and foundational properties.

A linkage, then, can have among its constituents not only participants, channels, props, and settings but also other linkages. We simply have to introduce appropriate terminology and work out the details. A linkage which has one or more linkages among its constituents will be called a *compound linkage*. This is distinguished from a *simple linkage*, which has no linkages among its constituents. When a linkage participates in a compound linkage, it will be called a *compound participant* in the compound linkage. The functional part that it plays in this compound linkage is called a *compound part*.

When a person communicates with a group, we can analyze what he is doing at several levels. For example, at one level there may be a simple linkage having the person and a department-store clerk as participants. At a higher level there would be a compound linkage having the person as a participant and the toy department, which is a simple linkage, as a compound participant. And at a still higher level there would be a larger compound linkage having the person as a participant and the department store, which is a compound linkage, as a larger compound participant. The several analyses will be systematically related and useful for different purposes.

And when two groups communicate with each other, as a city government and a public utility company, this can also be analyzed on several levels down to the two individuals talking to each other on the telephone.

A community can be analyzed from this point of view as a complex multiple hierarchy of linkages and compound linkages. An individual is seen as participating in very many of these linkages and compound linkages, which cover all of the significant structurings of the community. This view does not have the tangled complexity of the linkage network view, or the extreme oversimplification of the covering linkage view. It models realistically the ways in which the community is actually structured communicatively, and thus allows us to develop a fuller understanding of how people communicate. This view of the relation of individual and community in human linguistics is thus quite different from the concept of an ideal speaker-listener in a completely homogeneous speech-community, which will be familiar to some readers.

On the basis of the present discussion it should be clear that a human linguistics is indeed possible, and that the second alternative is indeed a feasible option. We are now ready to move on and test some further implications of the theory against observational evidence, and in so doing to compare the prospects of human linguistics with the past performance of business as usual.

CHAPTER TEN

Tests of Theory against Observation

A reader with a pragmatic turn of mind may admit that Bloomfield's assumption is unjustified but ask: What's the matter with that? What practical difference does it make? It has been quite serviceable, so why not just retain it and continue with business as usual?

One cannot so easily dismiss the issue of intellectual integrity at the very core of the discipline in regard to the incompatibility of grammar and science and in regard to the psychological and social reality of grammar fallacies. Nor can one easily dismiss the fact that the foundations of traditional theory are based on an unjustified assumption and must therefore be rejected by science, whereas the foundations of human linguistics are based on observationally supported general laws and therefore meet the most stringent scientific requirements.

But it does also make a considerable practical difference as well. A number of specific issues and problems have arisen in the everyday conduct of linguistic research that are a direct result of these core conceptual difficulties. They follow from trying to understand observations obtained from people in terms of concepts of language and grammar, and in trying to adhere simultaneously to the incompatible goals of studying language, of being scientific, and of seeking explanations in terms of people.

We will now examine or reexamine several sorts of easily available observational evidence and compare its treatment in human linguistics and in business as usual. This will amount to a comparison of the two bodies of theory in terms of how well they agree with the evidence. At the same time this will allow us to gain a further understanding of the architecture of human linguistics and its relation to more familiar theories.

The interpretation of the evidence will be clear if we renew our commitment to science and use only scientific criteria in making judgments about linguistic theory. Decisions regarding the details of linguistic theory, or even what brand of linguistic theory to accept, have too often been colored by personal preference, aesthetic considerations, adherence to tradition, or allegiance to a school of grammar. By relying instead on the criteria of science, we can use external objective evidence. Then such decisions will more resemble scientific judgments about whether the earth is flat or round, whether water is an element or a compound, or whether malaria is caused by bad air or is transmitted by mosquitoes.

The evidence to be presented seems to be generally accepted, indeed incontrovertible.

THE SCOPE OF PHENOMENA COVERED

Before looking at the evidence in detail, let us reexamine the question of the scope of observations that are of interest. The scope of a discipline is to some extent arbitrary, depending on the focus and breadth of interest of the investigators and the range of the questions they are initially asking. But a science may also be guided by theoretical considerations. If certain observations initially appear to be interrelated, it may prove fruitful to seek additional related observations in the hope of interconnecting them by means of an appropriate unifying theory. As various investigations are carried out and various theories are explored, the scope of the discipline may fluctuate. Then ultimately, when theory becomes more settled, the scope of the discipline will be seen more in terms of the scope of current theory than in terms of the initial range of the questions asked.

Can the broad scope of linguistics laid out in chapter 2 be justified on the basis of perceived interrelations of the observations? In support of a broad scope it is sometimes pointed out (Pike 1967:30) that different types of communicative behavior may be substitutable or partially substitutable. Clearly there are cases where speech and writing are substitutable: One can call a person on the telephone or write a letter instead. Gestures and speech are sometimes substitutable: There are clear gestures for *Good-bye*, *Come here*, *May I have one?*, *Look over there*, *Yes*, *No*, and others. Furthermore, when such gestures accompany speech there are constraints of appropriateness resembling the familiar phenomena of grammaticality. There are methods of signing used by the deaf that substitute for speech. In terms of signs and symbols one need only point to standard international traffic and highway signs, such as for *No parking*, and standard international signs to mark restaurants, rest rooms, access for the handicapped, etc. In the area of clothing, uniforms, and badges, one can see substitutes for an explicit spoken introduction or announcement of the person's occupation, rank, or position. Foote (1983) has studied color usage in the facades of public buildings using a human linguistics perspective. He has shown that facades can be seen as indicating to the public the type of organization housed in the building (bank, church, expensive restaurant, cheap restaurant), and that this in a sense substitutes for a barker out front announcing what is inside the building.

Traditional linguistic theory cannot cover such a broad scope. It represents the end point of a long series of investigations focused first on philosophical questions in the area of logic and the theory of knowledge, and second on specifying how to speak and write the language with propriety. These endeavors have bequeathed to us a traditional scope defined in terms of grammatical theory, a scope that has seemed too narrow to encompass all the phenomena of interest. Efforts to broaden the scope in semiotics have run into difficulties in how to accommodate the vast richness of detail confronted by grammatical theory without the narrowness of grammatical theory.

Human linguistics has a scope that covers the full range of verbal and nonverbal communicative phenomena and at the same time it provides a nongrammatical theoretical structure that can accommodate the full complexity of verbal communicative behavior.

THE FACTS OF VARIATION

Let us first review a point of observation already made: We observe that everyone is different. No two people we study speak exactly alike, and no one person speaks the same at different times. This has been recognized by virtually every leading linguist for the last century and a half, and can easily be tested to any reasonable degree of certainty.

We also observe that different people are partially alike. For any two people, or any one person at different times, similarities can be observed. This is not as often emphasized, but it is just as true, and can also be put to the test.

The observed communicative similarities of people are not as often remarked as the differences, for the traditional concept of language has always implied uniformity. For example, uniformity was implied in Bloomfield's assumption through the concept of a speech-community, which was defined as those who speak the same language. Traditional theories have treated observed similarities as simply reflecting the assumed uniformity, and then have had the problem of trying to explain or explain away the differences. This has caused a long series of practical problems in the conduct of linguistic research, particularly research on variation and on historical change.

Early linguists developed the comparative method on the twin tacit assumptions of uniform languages and sudden splits; individual variation was attributed to individual style and free will (Schleicher 1850:24), and thus its consideration was placed outside of linguistics. Saussure attributed similarities to langue but made individual variation a part of parole, which he did not treat, even though he recognized that it was the source of language change. But the assumptions underlying the comparative method of uniform languages and sudden splits proved not to correspond well with the historical evidence.

In dialect geography there was initial surprise that sharp lines of demarcation could not be found between different dialects. Then it was found that even with individual speech-sounds it was impossible to find sharp lines of demarcation, and even with the pronunciation of a single word an isogloss could not be drawn, as usage often fluctuated over a wider area.

Recently such problems have been magnified in trying to deal with observations of creole situations and of social variation using concepts of dialect that imply uniformity. Bloomfield was aware of the problems and produced many paragraphs explaining that the term speech-community has only a relative value (1933:54). Yet he did not abandon it, and an assumption of perfectly uniform speech-communities is sometimes still explicitly made even today, in spite of frequent objections from those who study variation. Perfectly uniform speech-communities are conceivable, but any scientific hypothesis of uniformity is refuted by over a century of field studies. The remarkable persistence of this idea in the face of such massive contradictory evidence attests to the degree to which the assumptions of the grammatical tradition have been ingrained into our culture by two millennia of normative grammar in the schools.

In science it is necessary to give priority to the evidence over traditional theory or a priori assumptions. If the evidence shows that any two people, or the same person at different times, are partly alike and partly different communicatively, and that any two groups are likewise partly alike and partly different, then we should have a theory that mirrors these observations, rather than one that reflects a uniformity that does not exist.

In human linguistics these observations of partial similarities and differences, rather than being ignored in the core theory, are actually taken as observational evidence supporting the most basic law in the foundations of the discipline: the law of componential partitioning, which makes available the concept of properties for use in research in human linguistics, and the methods of sames and differents already familiar in the other domain. With the concept of properties, a human-linguistic theory of groups has at hand a ready apparatus for handling variation of all sorts and for understanding communication between individuals who are different in some respects and the same in other respects.

Much of the recent work on variation, creole studies, and sociolinguistics has focused on linguistic differences and has provided valuable evidence and insights that could be carried over rather easily into the human-linguistics framework. It would require recasting the results into the form of postulated properties of individuals and statements of the distribution of these properties over the population studied. Some of the published data are already almost in this form; for example, Bickerton (1973) reports data on several points of usage by a number of speakers of Guyanese creole, keeping the observed usage of different speakers separate. Then group properties could be postulated and various simple and compound linkages set up to try to capture the social and community phenomena underlying the data. It should be possible to retain the best insights of creole continua and wave-theory accounts while eliminating some of their difficulties.

Furthermore, with methods available for handling contextual factors in the individual in a straightforward way, there is the possibility of explicitly accounting for the sociolinguistic factors operating in the individual that underlie the choice between variant forms. One could then account for variation within the same individual. And when individuals with quite different properties communicate through a pidgin, it can be understood through the concepts of role part and participant how they can do the same thing in quite different ways.

Besides ridding the studies of unsupported assumptions, this course would provide additional insight through a clearer separation of individual and social phenomena, and the possibility of working out the interesting and intricate linguistic interrelations between the individual and the group or society that he participates in. Such attempts would undoubtedly raise new questions requiring the gathering of additional observational evidence.

INTUITIONS AND THE CORRECTION OF MISTAKES

It is observed that while people are speaking they sometimes stop and correct themselves. When asked, they generally acknowledge that they misspoke or that they made an error. They can also often be observed to correct their own writing.

Further, people can express opinions about whether a given utterance is something that they would say or something that they would not say, or whether it is correct or not, or according to good usage or not, or whether it is something that one can say in the language or not. Such judgments are often carefully elicited by linguists for use as grammaticality judgments, and are a major source of evidence for linguistic research in business as usual.

It is also observed that the judgments of different people differ as to what one can say in the language or not. Field linguists are also well aware that what people report that they would or would not say often does not correspond with what they do in fact habitually say, even when there is no question of their having misspoken or made a mistake.

In the normative tradition, such opinions were seen as reflecting views concerning a prescriptive norm. Differences of opinion were settled by reference to authority. Grammarians sometimes trusted their own judgment and intuitions, or more often followed older authorities or the usage of prestigious literary figures or eminent personages. Most people relied on the authority of grammars, style manuals, and dictionaries. And they still do. Thus it did not strike one as odd that people would make mistakes, especially in view of the fact that the road to knowledge was through literacy, and the road to literacy was through grammar taught in grammar school. The model of the speaker or writer could easily be seen as the schoolchild or still insecure adult struggling with Latin, or with some other standard language differing from his own speech, and inevitably making mistakes.

Then when grammarians in the new discipline of linguistics ceased being lawgivers and became instead scientists describing a language, the concept of language as normative was set aside, but the assumption that it was an ideal of perfection was retained. And for those who also accepted the assumption of the social or psychological reality of grammar, this ideal was given a social or psychological embodiment. Thus for Saussure language was not complete in any speaker; it existed perfectly only in a collectivity: it was a grammatical system having only a potential existence in each brain, and he spoke in terms of the metaphors of the rules of chess or the score for an orchestral work as ideals of perfection separate and distinct from the tactics of the chess player or the interpretations or mistakes of the musicians. For Chomsky, on the other hand, language was not embodied in a collectivity but in an assumed paragon, ''an ideal speaker-listener in a completely homogeneous speech-community, who knows its language perfectly and is unaffected by such grammatically irrelevant conditions as memory limitations, distractions, shifts of attention and interest, and errors (random or characteristic) in applying his knowledge of the language in actual performance'' (Chomsky 1965:3).[1] The speaker-listener was hypothesized to have a linguistic competence mirroring this ideal of perfection, and this competence could be tapped by studying grammatical intuitions as revealed in grammaticality judgments. In this view, the object of study in linguistics was to be the competence of the ideal speaker-listener, not mere performance, which was marred by errors and other deviations that should be of no interest to the linguist. However, competence was supposed to underlie performance.

A number of cogent criticisms of this view may be found in the literature, among them that it does not adequately take into account that different people have different intuitions, there being no way of resolving the differences. Also one cannot obtain scientific evidence about competence. Since all of our evidence comes from mere mortals who are doomed to make errors, we are not able to test claims about the ideal speaker-listener's language or grammar. If actual speakers do not conform to a proposed ideal, the differences between theory and observation could be brushed aside as due to irrelevant performance factors, thus making the theory untestable and therefore unscientific.

The assumption that information about linguistic "competence" can be obtained from speaker's intuitions also has problems. If competence refers to knowledge of community norms and standards, there is the problem that in fact different speakers (and different linguists) have different intuitions. If it is assumed that competence refers to the speaker's own internal grammar, we run into the psychological reality of grammar fallacy. If competence is assumed to underlie performance, there is the problem that informant's reports of what they say are often at variance from what they do regularly say. And with only one standard, competence cannot account for mistakes. Since the theory cannot account for mistakes, their study has been rejected along with the study of variation and the differences between the individual and the community. This raises serious questions as to the actual relevance of data from intuitions, and casts considerable doubt on the concept of competence.

We have to conclude that neither the older nor the newer traditionally oriented theories do a very good job of confronting the evidence on intuitions and on the correction of mistakes.

In human linguistics the strong intuitions that speakers have of uniformity in the speech-community and of accepted community norms and standards are predicated of the individuals, who project them as stereotypes on themselves, on others, and on the community. Since in this theory all individuals are different we can easily handle the observations that different people have different stereotypes, and since there is also a theory of groups, we can study and analyze the properties of the community itself and compare these findings with the different stereotypes. We can also analyze the single individual from several points of view: On the basis of observational evidence we can postulate properties responsible for what the individual actually does when he speaks. On the basis of evidence from "errors" that are corrected, we can postulate other properties at a different level responsible for the observed monitoring and corrective behavior. Then we can face the separate issue of whether the individual properties implied by informant responses on intuitions, projections, and stereotypes actually coincide or not with the properties responsible for the "mistakes" or the properties responsible for the "corrections."

DYNAMIC ASPECTS OF COMMUNICATIVE BEHAVIOR

Next let us look at some additional observational evidence already mentioned, evidence that is so obvious that it seems banal. Yet there have been difficulties in accommodating it in business as usual. It is observed that communicative behavior is a dynamic process that takes place in time. When people speak, or when they communicate in other ways, their positions and movements change with time, and these cause energy flows such as sound waves and reflected light that change with time. Since people and the energy flows exist in the real world, this may seem unsurprising. But not every object in the real world shows such complex and highly structured temporal changes. It is not only individual persons that show changes with time as they communicate. Groups of persons also show changes with time as the people making up the group communicate with each other. Why has it been so difficult to accommodate these elementary observational facts?

Grammar provides an inherently static picture, a presumed relation between sound and meaning. Grammar answers to static data, such as judgments of well-formedness or grammaticality. The grammatical analysis of a sentence has sometimes been described rather aptly as a marble-slab approach. Grammar does not model physical processes taking place in time; it was not designed for that purpose.

However, the use of process terms that invoke a dynamic metaphor when talking about static grammar has been a continuing source of confusion. The ancient processes of addition, deletion, substitution, and transposition have led in modern times to process terms being applied almost everywhere in linguistics. Terms like "transform" and "generate" are the hallmark of modern generative and transformational approaches, which are characterized by rules of grammar that are applied to yield "outputs."

If one does not take this talk metaphorically, a number of questions are raised. In what domain do linguistic processes take place? In what realm are the intermediate results of a derivation to be found? Who applies grammatical rules? Are they rules to be consulted by writers or editors in normalizing a text as in prescriptive grammar? Are they rules of calculation applied by the linguist in deducing the consequences of his theory? Are they like rules of logic or rules of algebra? Are they simply a way of writing down assumed relations between assumed linguistic entities? The issue is seldom faced explicitly in the linguistics literature. Instead one finds the agent suppressed by use of the passive, a nominalization, or other means: *this rule is applied . . . , the rule application . . . , this rule produces. . . .*

Because many linguists are basically interested in people, there has been an almost irresistible urge to try to account for what people do by assuming that grammar rules control communicative behavior when people speak and understand. Most linguists, including the author, have succumbed to this urge at one time or another. This is in spite of the admonitions of eminent linguists, which are regularly repeated, and in spite of the widespread understanding that to make such an assumption would be to ignore a fallacy. Grammar rules do not model the flow of time in the physical sense. They would have to have a physical embodiment if their execution controlled behavior. Grammar rules are in the logical domain, not the physical. There is a greater gulf between these two domains than the gulf between soul and body in Descartes's thinking. Not only would we run into the psychological and social reality of grammar fallacies, but we would be tempted to institute a fruitless search for some pineal-gland principle to connect competence and performance.

In human linguistics, observations of the physical positions and motions of people when they communicate, and the observed effects of communicative behavior on noncommunicative behavior, constitute the physical evidence behind the theory. Human-linguistic theory does model the flow of time in the physical sense. It models the physical reality of people, individually and collectively, from the point of view of how they communicate. The dynamic aspects of speaking and understanding are accounted for in terms of the execution of procedures under the control of the conditional properties.

Procedures are not like rules. A rule is usually thought of as something a person can apply or not as he sees fit, like a normative rule, and thus a speaker could make a mistake and not apply the rule, or he could deliberately ignore the rule if he wished. Under this conception the rules do not account for mistakes and the grammar does not account for deliberate violations. A procedure, on the other hand, is a part of a scientific theory of the person or group, postulated to account for the observed communicative behavior of the person or group. Whether a procedure executes or not depends on the state of the individual at that point, also postulated to account for observed communicative behavior.

True, there may be some carry-over of theoretical results from phrase-structure conceptions into a structure of task procedures and selection procedures. This can aid in the further development of human-linguistic theory and help to preserve valid insights already gained. Phrase-structure approaches to grammar promise to be more helpful than transformational approaches. But although the phrase structure of a sentence sometimes resembles the structure of the nested task procedures carried out when an individual speaks or understands, sometimes there are differences. Since the two theoretical structures rest on quite different foundations, considerable care will have to be exercised so as not to introduce unsupported assumptions and erroneous results.

REFERENTIAL PHENOMENA

If one nevertheless presses on with business as usual, ignoring the problems already discussed, more problems emerge in trying to account for frequent and familiar observations. Among the most pressing are problems of ambiguity in reference. Let us look at some of the evidence:

A frequently cited example is the word *bank*, which can mean a financial institution or the edge of a river. However a glance at a dictionary will reveal that most words are listed with multiple meanings. The word *run* is perhaps the extreme case in English. Yet we are usually not confused by this when we talk or listen to others, and generally understand what is intended in spite of the many seeming ambiguities. How do we manage to communicate effectively in the face of these apparently insurmountable difficulties?

Another puzzling area has been pronominal reference. Words like *he*, *it*, *they*, and *you*, continually shift their reference, designating different people or things at different times. For this reason they have sometimes been called shifters. Yet in actual conversation we are rarely confused as to what person or thing is being referred to. How can we account for this?

A possibly related and well-known phenomenon is that a single word to a close friend may often be sufficient for what would require a long explanation with a casual acquaintance. How can we understand this fact?

Such observations are difficult to understand and to account for in business as usual because the linguistics of language has been based on traditional sign theory. Since in this theory words signify concepts, there is a presumption that signifiers stand in one-to-one relation to the things signified. This would be important in a theory of knowledge, where ambiguity could not be tolerated, and it is still widely considered to be the standard case from which deviations must be explained. The problem of ambiguity was considered at length by the ancients and has given rise to an extensive literature in modern times. It is often said that the answer to the ease of resolution of ambiguity in ordinary discourse rests in the context. This does little more than give the problem a name: the problem of context. How can we take the context into account?

The ancients introduced the concept of grammatical level to explain observations of ambiguity. They pointed out that an item that was ambiguous at the lower level of diction (*lexis*) was not ambiguous at the higher level of speech (*logos*). A standard Stoic example was equivalent to the familiar pair *a name*, *an aim*, which sound alike at one level but are different at a higher level. Modern linguists use similar arguments to introduce transformational or other levels. But this device has only limited usefulness in dealing with the general problem of ambiguity.

Some modern attempts postulate operations of scanning back and forth in the surrounding text for clues that would resolve ambiguities. Context is thus seen as the surrounding text. Some cases can be handled in this way. But the whole enterprise breaks down with the more difficult examples such as pronominal reference to something not yet mentioned, pronominal reference to something not previously expressed in a single word or phrase, and especially cases where a single word between close friends suffices for what would require a long explanation with others. And no good explanations are at hand for how a person can distinguish which sense of *bank* or of *run* was intended by the speaker.

One has to conclude that after 2,000 years of effort, traditional approaches to the problem of ambiguity and to reference in general are still less than satisfactory and leave many questions unanswered and many puzzles unresolved. The reason for this is that traditional sign theory provides no conceptual apparatus for taking the context into account, and neither does grammatical theory, which descended from it.

Human linguistics, on the other hand, does offer a means in its underlying structure for taking the context into account: At any given point in time the context is represented in the conditional properties. During communicative behavior the conditional properties of the individual in the domain of control are continually changing, constituting the changing context of situation for the individual. And it is the changing conditional properties that help to control the dynamic processes of producing and understanding communicative behavior. Thus an analysis of the individual in terms of properties automatically includes an analysis of the effect of the context of situation on communicative behavior.

If the speaker and hearer have sufficient commonality of properties, the speaker will produce signals that will trigger appropriate changes in the conditional properties of the listener that represent correct understanding. If the speaker and hearer do not at the moment have sufficient commonality of properties, the signal produced will be inappropriate or ineffective for the hearer, and a misunderstanding or a lack of understanding will occur. Thus there is the possibility of our being able to analyze not only understanding but misunderstanding as well. Although the detailed analysis of properties in human linguistics is only at its beginning, there is nothing in principle standing in the way of accounting for the evidence given above and other evidence of a similar sort.

In a discussion of philosophical views of referring, Linsky (1967:116) has said that it is the users of language who refer, not expressions. Although the concept of users of language is problematic, this statement is correct in that it points to people as the locus of the phenomena. To achieve a scientific understanding of referring, we need a theory of people, not a theory of expressions, words, or signs.

DISCOURSE PHENOMENA

Considerable attention of late has been paid to phenomena of discourse. Such studies have gone under the name of the study of dialog, the study of conversation, face-to-face interaction, discourse analysis, and text linguistics.

Typical among the phenomena are those related to question-answer sequences, the topic of conversation, the thread of conversation, the organization of stories, and negotiation and agreement in dialog.

Attempts have been made to confront these phenomena with apparatus similar to the apparatus of grammar. Concepts of cohesion and coherence of discourse have been modeled on concepts of grammaticality of sentences, and efforts have been made to discover the devices of cohesion, such as various types of connective words, pronouns, and the like. Difficulties have shown up due to the assumed constraints of cohesion across sentence boundaries appearing not to be as strong as the constraints of grammar and syntax within the domain of a sentence, and the suspicion that cohesive phenomena may be of a different nature altogether from grammatical phenomena.

Some of the most interesting results coming from these studies have to do with the realization of the importance of the situational context and attempts at taking it into account. It is often assumed that when a topic of conversation is established, or a question is up for discussion, or an agreement has been reached, that the topic, the question, or the agreement "exist in the conversation." This has the problem that it offers no means for analyzing cases where the different parties to the conversation are talking to slightly different topics or discussing slightly different questions, or differ as to whether agreement has been reached. It is an advance over purely text-based ideas, however, because the topic, the question, or the agreement is assumed to be currently salient rather than existing in the prior text that set it up. It could thus affect the current course of the conversation directly without our having to assume some routines of scanning back into the previous text for an indefinite distance. This is the advantage of a state approach, but it needs to be anchored in reality, for something "existing in the conversation" is at best only in the logical or grammatical domain, and therefore not actually available to affect what a conversationalist does next.

In human linguistics the topic, the question, or the agreement would exist first in the state properties of each individual, that is, remembered in their conditional properties, and therefore available to affect what each may say or do next by helping to control which procedures are executed. The topic, question, or agreement need not be identically represented in the properties of the different individuals. In human linguistics the topic, the question, or the agreement can also be analyzed at the group or linkage level. It takes at least two people to agree, to disagree, or to negotiate, and the linkage can have properties of agreement or disagreement in the group, or of a continuing state of negotiation. Thus in human linguistics the context of situation is embedded in the properties of the individuals and linkages rather than being a free-floating abstraction.[2]

PRAGMATIC PHENOMENA

Pragmatic phenomena have excited considerable interest in recent years. It is observed that by means of speech signals people can make promises, seal bargains, make bets, and christen ships. They can do such things as warning, commanding, asking, requesting. They can carry out many other everyday activities simply by means of speech or other communicative behavior.

To this one should add phenomena of cooperation. It can be observed that the exchange of communicative signals such as speech serves to coordinate social activities of all sorts, from the family to friendships to activities in the workplace to shopping to participation in all the public and private entities that a person is associated with.

Pragmatic phenomena were seen as anomalous from the point of view of theories that placed emphasis on logic and the idea that sentences express propositions that can be judged true or false (Austin 1962). Attempts have been made by philosophers and linguists to treat such phenomena in a pragmatic theory, and a number of interesting insights have been gained. The effort, however, has had many problems well known to those who have followed the literature. These problems are usually related to the retention of traditional concepts of language. For example, when someone makes a promise to someone else, what really happens? A discussion rooted in the domain of language and grammar does not offer satisfactory answers.

A distinction between syntax, semantics, and pragmatics was formulated by Morris (1938:6) and Carnap (1942:9). According to this distinction, investigations that make explicit reference to the user of a language are in the field of pragmatics. If they abstract from the user of the language and analyze only the expressions and their designata (i.e., what is referred to), they are in the field of semantics. If they abstract from the designata also and analyze only the relations between the expressions, they are in the field of (logical) syntax. Thus in this view semantics includes syntax, and pragmatics includes both semantics and syntax. This conception, on the face of it, appears to surmount the barrier between the domain of logic and language and the domain of people, and to move in the direction of a human linguistics.

Linguistics owes a debt of gratitude to Austin and the others who have explored pragmatic phenomena for opening up a field of study and raising new questions that demand answers. In continuing to assume objects of language and grammar, the program instituted has retained strong ties to the grammatical tradition in the logical domain. This has initially appeared to tie the work in pragmatics to earlier work, thus increasing its apparent relevance to other linguistic concerns. Many pragmatic studies thus paradoxically continue to abstract away from people by introducing additional assumed entities such as speech acts, or they interpret their results as providing information on what people do with words or how people use language. But it has not been clear what kind of a conception of words or of language would support the idea that they could be *used* by someone for some purpose. Again we run into the psychological and social reality of grammar fallacies.

If pragmatics includes both semantics and syntax, the distinction introduced in earlier years as an a priori programmatic partitioning of the domain of study may no longer be necessary. A restructuring may be possible and appropriate. Human linguistics is that restructuring: it moves the treatment of all the phenomena over from the logical side of the barrier to the physical side. Thus human linguistics can be viewed as pragmatics freed from any ties to signs, language, and grammar.[3]

Such a restructuring on the human side is also necessary if pragmatics is to mature, to cut the apron strings, as so many other fields of inquiry have done, and move away from philosophy to accept the discipline and control of science. The reason for this is simply that people are a part of nature, observable, and given in advance, while the objects of logic and language are not.

In human linguistics we can say that when someone makes a promise, his state properties change in ways that can be verified by observing his subsequent behavior in keeping the promise, and the state properties of the person to whom he has made the promise also change in ways that affect his future observable behavior. He expects the promise to be kept, and if it is not kept he may complain or even institute a lawsuit. Thus the state of having made a promise and the state of having been promised are of the very nature that human linguistics has been designed to handle with its concept of conditional properties, and there is a mechanism in the procedural properties for understanding how these states affect future observable behavior. Furthermore, human linguistics treats phenomena that have previously been seen as semantic, syntactic, even phonological, by these same means, that is, in terms of the properties of the people involved and their changes. Human linguistics can be viewed as a linguistic theory that has been moved to the physical domain so that it can be pragmatic from top to bottom.

PHENOMENA OF METAPHOR AND FIGURATIVE LANGUAGE

Having come this far in understanding the influence of context, we are ready to consider some observational evidence that has seemed even more puzzling: the phenomena usually referred to as figurative language. Perhaps the most perplexing have been the phenomena of metaphor, where it is said that a word or phrase literally meaning one thing is used to refer to something different so as to suggest a likeness or analogy between the two things, and of irony, where a word or phrase may be used to express the opposite of its literal meaning.

Such phenomena have seemed anomalous from the point of view of traditional theories. How can we understand that a word can mean something that it doesn't mean, or even just the opposite, in a theory of signs with an assumed norm of one word one meaning?

Of the four ancient processes, substitution has sometimes been suggested in attempted explanations: it is assumed that the word used has been substituted for the word meant on the basis of some principle of similarity or relatedness—no real explanation. Some modern grammarians have suggested that there are degrees of grammaticality, with metaphor being semigrammatical. But the phenomena seem to be semantic in nature rather than grammatical or syntactic. Some logicians have suggested that metaphors are simply false, or else trivially true, yet logic is incapable of accounting for the phenomena. These are but a few of the suggestions that have been put forward: the literature on metaphor is as vast as it is diverse and scientifically unsatisfactory.

Another of the ancient processes, deletion (ellipsis), has sometimes been invoked in explanations of metaphor. Metaphor would be an elliptical simile: *War is like hell* → *War is hell*; *He's like a prince* → *He's a prince*. But it would be more difficult to treat adequately in this way Plato's metaphor as quoted in Aristotle's *Poetics* 21: *Old age is the sunset of life*. There are several problems with explanations assuming a process of ellipsis. If the assumption of the objects of language and grammar such as speech-sounds, words, and phrases is unjustified, the status of objects of language assumed and then deleted is even more tenuous. Using this principle, even irony could be handled by deletion of *but I mean just the opposite*. This point is related to objections raised against deletion transformations on the basis that they would make the grammar too powerful.

The appeal to ellipsis is at least as old as the second century (Apollonius Dyscolus), but it seems more like a fudge or a clever trick than an explanation: When the analysis of an expression is difficult in a theory inadequate to handle the context of situation, assume some clarifying text (or its equivalent in underlying form) overtly expressing the needed situational context, handle the whole thing with traditional methods for handling text, then delete the clarifying text.

In human linguistics all dynamic processes are hypothesized as carried out in systems modeling real objects—people. Such hypotheses are not immune to test in the way that assumptions of ellipsis in an assumed domain of language or grammar would be.

When traditional theory would assume that some process of ellipsis has deleted things that are "understood but not expressed," human linguistics would treat them as being in the salient context of situation represented in the conditional properties of the people involved. Here they are available to contribute to the understanding of metaphor and irony. These properties are set up and changed over the length of a conversation or even an acquaintanceship. Thus they may have been set up at times arbitrarily distant in the past, and problems associated with taking the surrounding words as the context do not arise. The processes by which these properties are made selectively salient at any given moment are complex but subject to linguistic investigation. An adequate treatment of the phenomena of figurative language would appear to require a dynamic theory of this type, for the understanding of a metaphor, like beauty, is in the mind of the beholder, and different people may exhibit different understandings when their relevant properties are different.

Much that has been written on topics of figurative language will be relevant for human linguistics. Works by humanistic scholars in the areas of literature and poetics in particular can be expected to contain valuable insights to be carried over. Social disciplines as well, such as area studies, social and cultural anthropology, and the history of civilizations, cultures, and institutions, are rich resources. In this vast literature the most insightful work is often also the least formalized. The keenest insights on metaphor come from the fields of rhetoric and literary criticism. Unhampered by a rigorous formalized theory, these authors have been free to speculate, contrive, and improvise. They have seen that the allusions involved in the phenomena of figurative language are personal and often idiosyncratic, and marked by extreme contextual dependence. Complex dynamic mental processes are required for their explanation. Human linguistics provides a dynamic state theory appropriate to this need that lends itself to formalization and careful scientific test against observational evidence.

Considering the difficulties of handling figurative language in the linguistics of language, it is no wonder that literary critics and others who are sensitive to the nuance and beauty in literature have not flocked to formal linguistics for theoretical underpinnings. But human linguistics can provide the formal apparatus they need. Thus by moving decidedly into the natural sciences, linguistics stands to make greater contributions to humanistic studies. This may seem paradoxical to those who have imagined some inherent incompatibility between the aims of the humanities and the methods of science. Human linguistics bridges what has sometimes been perceived as a wide gap by providing a greater insight into the human mechanisms underlying the poetic and artistic qualities we value so highly in the best writing.

THE SOCIAL IMPLICATIONS OF COMMUNICATIVE BEHAVIOR

A number of interesting observations about communicative phenomena in small social groups have been reported by the sociologist Erving Goffman. His insightful work and the work of others on the study of collective behavior deals with face-to-face interaction in everyday activities. It concentrates on the communicative glue so intimately involved in ordinary gatherings and encounters in a society. The work treats such topics as situated activity, games, rituals, performances, and the allocation of involvement. It is concerned with deference, situational proprieties and improprieties, embarrassment, alienation, face, role, and being in character. There is no doubt that these phenomena have a heavy communicative component and are very important for any scientific study of how people communicate. An entry into the work of this prolific writer can be made through Goffman (1963).

Goffman's work describes the phenomena so vividly that the reader recognizes things out of his own experience that he has never noticed before or seen in this light. Like the broad-ranging observations of the great naturalists of the 19th century, it has revealed the phenomena to our eyes. This is a necessary first step; one needs to be able to see something before one can study it. The next step would be to study the phenomena more closely and try to test the claims that have been made.

Although the insights presented are usually intuitively obvious and perhaps correct, one cannot rely on the intuitions of readers as adequate tests for the validity of scientific claims. One would need more formal and objective tests. For this it will be necessary to state the claims in precise terms, that is, to formalize them. But no means of formalization has been provided.

Neither traditional linguistic theory nor modern formal linguistics provide support for treating such observations. They completely lack any apparatus suited to confronting phenomena of this order. Thus the linguistics of language is largely innocent of any connection with social communicative phenomena. Undoubtedly for this reason work like Goffman's is equally innocent of any connection with traditional linguistic or grammatical theory. Here we have two disciplines, current sociology and current linguistics in business as usual, both dealing centrally with human communication, and they are as separate as two islands.

Human linguistics does provide the necessary formal apparatus. It was designed not only to solve the problems facing grammatical approaches but also to be adequate for formalizing the sorts of insights we have from people like Goffman. In fact Goffman's work was a great stimulus in the development of the human linguistic theory of groups. Linkage theory in particular can be used for formalizing various concepts of groups, engagements, and encounters in terms of their properties in a dynamic theory. And the concepts of participant, role part, and role type are suitable for formalizing the involvements of the individual in terms of properties. Then we will be ready for large-scale formalization of work in this area and careful research aimed at enlarging the scope of validated scientific knowledge in the social sciences.

WRITING AND THE ADVANCEMENT OF KNOWLEDGE

Let us end by looking at another aspect of communication that is beyond the capabilities of the linguistics of language. This is the physical-domain social and cultural role of writing in modern societies. Writing has been extremely important in the advancement of knowledge and the rise of modern civilizations. Written material is the repository for much of our culture and an agent of its propagation to succeeding generations.

In human linguistics, writing can be considered as a type of channel in a linkage, or the written material can be analyzed as props that directly couple different linkages. In either case one of its most salient characteristics is the usual separation in time and space of the two participants, the writer and the reader.

This separation introduces a delay and the impossibility of immediate responses. Understanding is relative to the reader, but the writer is denied feedback as to the changing state properties of the reader as he reads and tries to understand. If the reader does not understand, he can only give further study to what has been written.

A writer is therefore well advised to be clearer and more explicit than he would need to be in a face-to-face interaction. This results inevitably in differences in style. And when the writing is directed not to a known person but to an unknown audience, the writer is less sure as to what he can assume on the part of the readers, and there is a concomitant pressure for the assumption of a standard audience and for developing standard ways of writing. This may be one of the reasons for the emergence of normative grammars, dictionaries, and style manuals, and the continuing need for them in modern society. These points seem quite obvious in human linguistics, but they cannot be discussed at all, much less tested scientifically, in the linguistics of language, which is often content to dismiss writing as merely secondary to speech.

What is the nature of the linkages involving books as props? The characteristics of delay open up the possibility of multiple readers through time. When a book has many readers, it serves as a prop in a linkage with each reader, and couples the linkages to each other with the broadcast type of coupling through contact in the prop. When the readers read the book, they develop commonality of properties. If a person reads many books he will be a participant in many such linkages that are coupled in this way to many other linkages. Note also that writers will refer to, allude to, or build on the work of others, thus expanding the circle connected to the reader. For some people linkages through writing vie in importance with personal contacts in relation to certain subject matters. In this way we begin to appreciate the nature of a literature and of an intellectual community or discipline. The human-linguistic theory of groups applies beautifully to these areas, for it has a conceptual structure of participants and props, direct and indirect coupling, and simple and compound linkages for treating overlapping and interacting groups organized around certain commonalities of properties.

The characteristics of delay also open up the possibility of storage and preservation for posterity. What exactly is it that is stored? We know, of course, that it is not just books that are stored. Some would say that it is "information," but then the debate begins as to what sort of thing "information" might be. In human linguistics the relativity of understanding to the readers as participants in linkages with the books as props becomes clear, and formal methods exist for precise analysis.

Note the freedom of association afforded to the individual by the availability of an open literature as provided by libraries. A person is free to set up his own linkages with the props. He can enter into any society of published scientists, scholars, and writers without invitation, and can participate in their intellectual culture. Already important in ancient times, the library has grown over the years to serve the functions of storing, preserving, organizing, and providing access to these materials until today we have multilibrary networks and huge computerized data banks all for handling the written word. These institutions are subject to analysis at every level in human linguistics terms, for the library is first and foremost an instrument of communication.

Knowledge has to do with a potentiality for taking action. But this requires having all the required knowledge in the same person. The main barrier to this is the immensity of the written record, which has given rise to specialization, with each person knowing only a fraction of the total. It is sometimes thought that if something is published, it thereby becomes "known." This raises the problem "known by whom?" If a person lacks certain needed knowledge, it is not always easy for him to find it even if he suspects it might exist. But if not, what is he to do? The result has been the often fortuitous aspect of progress in scientific research, the adventitious direct contact between linkages in a scientist as a participant in both. A report in *Science* (Lewin 1985) states that "owing to the fortuitous combination of two diverse interests—those of slime mold biology and the habits of migratory songbirds—in a Princeton researcher . . . one curious aspect of this natural history appears to have been solved.''

The vastness of the printed record points up the importance of organization for retrieval. The difficulty of looking something up that one doesn't know exists has led to reviews of the literature and encyclopedias. A report on a biology-wide computerized information system summarized in the same issue of *Science* (Holden 1985) suggests that better organization of existing information may well yield new knowledge.

So much for science. What about the humanities? What about novels, short stories, poems? What about history? Some of the same considerations hold here as well, particularly the adventitious nature of a person's background, which gives him a view of culture unique to himself. The uniqueness of the individual is central in human linguistics, figuring importantly in the very foundations of the theoretical structure. Philological and literary applications can be foreseen, and aid in understanding the nature of popular culture and the media, which are very important for determining the direction and values of society.

One problem the individual sometimes has in communicating with others and in confronting the written record is the language barrier. Human linguistics holds potentialities for understanding the nature of bilingualism in the individual and in the community. And it also will have much to say about translation, which takes place in the contact between linkages in the translator. The importance of translation in the modern world is clear when we remember that all communication between different linguistic areas must take place through individuals that are to some extent bilingual.

Other points of comparison could also be brought forward between the promise of human linguistics and the past performance of the linguistics of language, such as developmental, historical, ecological, evolutionary, and genetic considerations, which deal with changes in properties, and where a treatment in terms of the linguistics of language involves a category mistake or the psychological or social reality of grammar fallacies. These comparisons would only reinforce the conclusions already reached.

While it must be admitted that the grammatical tradition is strongly entrenched after 2000 years, the human-linguistics approach shows considerable promise already in its infancy. It would seem worthwhile to nurture it with care in the hope that as it matures it will help us to achieve a deeper and fuller understanding of how people communicate.

NOTES

1. QUESTIONS AND CLUES

1. The number of existing divergent grammatical positions has grown quite large. Parret (1974) contrasts the approaches of Wallace L. Chafe, Noam Chomsky, Algirdas J. Greimas, M. A. K. Halliday, Peter Hartmann, George Lakoff, Sydney M. Lamb, André Martinet, James McCawley, and Sebastian K. Shaumyan. But besides these there are also N. D. Andreev, Renate Bartsch, Irena Bellert, Manfred Bierwisch, Dwight Bolinger, M. K. Brame, Eugenio Coseriu, R. M. W. Dixon, Charles Fillmore, James Foley, Bruce Fraser, Gerald Gazdar, Bennison Gray, Zellig Harris, Charles Hockett, Richard Hudson, Esa Itkonen, Lauri Karttunen, Asa Kasher, Edward Keenen, Ronald W. Langaker, Hans-Heinrich Lieb, Igor A. Mel'čuk, Richard Montague, David Perlmutter, Kenneth Pike, Randolph Quirk, Petr Sgall, David Stampe, Teun A. van Dijk, Theo Vennemann, and Jef Verschueren, among others.

2. LANGUAGE AND LINGUISTICS

1. Thus when Galileo observed mountains and craters on the moon, and measured their heights and depths from the lengths of the shadows, one of his opponents, holding the ancient assumption that the moon must be a perfect sphere, suggested that the real moon is encased in a perfectly smooth and perfectly spherical crystal through which Galileo saw mountains and craters and was deceived into thinking that the surface was rough. Galileo replied that he would grant his adversary the use of this perfectly transparent crystalline substance provided his adversary with equal courtesy would allow him to construct of it mountains ten times as high and craters ten times as deep as those he had observed (Drake 1976:70).

2. A striking example is the case of Horne Tooke (1736–1812), who achieved a great social and intellectual reputation as the discoverer of the truth about language and its relation to thought and the mind. He dominated English philology for two generations with etymological nonsense based on "general reasoning à priori" in support of philosophical preconceptions and maintained by early ecstatic reviews, political acceptance, largely unquestioned personal authority, and the abuse and contempt which he poured on other positions (Aarsleff 1967).

3. This is not the place to enter into a discussion of the program and methods of modern science; some knowledge of these matters will be assumed in what follows. Students sometimes ask how to learn more about science. The best way is to study science under scientists. A major advantage of doing this is to undergo the process of socialization as a scientist. This is important because it is difficult to learn these things simply through reading. But lacking an opportunity to study under scientists, the least that one should do is to read science and the history of science (not the philosophy of science). A good place to start would be the essays on Galileo and translations of Galileo's works by Stillman Drake.

A surprising number of linguists read philosophy and the philosophy of science for instruction in how to do linguistics. This is fine for those who see linguistics as a branch of philosophy. But in the present work we see linguistics instead as a branch of science, and for this it is advisable that one learn science directly from scientists. Philosophy has important contributions to make, but teaching science is not one of them. Because the focus of philosophical works is on philosophical issues, their study is inappropriate preparation for someone trying to learn to be a scientist, and is likely to lead to confusions and misconceptions.

4. Some of the important positions of certain influential linguists will be touched on here. In many cases earlier versions of these positions may be found in the writings of their predecessors.

5. Thus it will be necessary to take just the opposite tack from that taken in Chomsky (1965:25): "Using the term 'grammar' with a systematic ambiguity (to refer, first, to the native speaker's internally represented 'theory of his language' and, second, to the linguist's account of this), we can say that the child has developed and internally represented a generative grammar, in the sense described." This appears to beg at least two important questions: whether a grammar is equivalent to the structure of people, and whether a theory is equivalent to what it purports to be a theory of.

3. ANALYSIS: THE DOMAIN OF LANGUAGE

1. Unfortunately none of the Stoic writings have been preserved intact. The existing fragmentary sources have been collected by Arnim (1903). Particularly valuable is the second century A.D. account of Diogenes Laertius (VII 39–83, especially 55–59). The Loeb edition (Hicks 1925) provides a convenient parallel English translation which, however, is not consistent in its rendering of the technical terms. A better translation into German is to be found in Egli (1967). See also Pinborg (1975), Robins (1951), Coseriu (1969) and Mates (1953). An annotated bibliography by Egli is to be found in Hülser (1979). The student will find differences between different accounts. If he turns to the sources, he will find them incomplete, sometimes cryptic and even contradictory.

2. Numerous quotations could be exhibited. Here are several from linguists who have been influential: "Die sprache ist ein naturobject, und die wissenschaft von ihr gleicht der naturgeschichte, welche der philosophischen betrachtung zwei objecte darbietet: 1) das verhältniss zwischen den einzelnen naturgegenständen: das system; 2) den bau der einzelnen körper und was dazu gehört: die physiologie" (Rask 1830 as quoted in Thomsen 1889:323). "Die Sprachwissenschaft hat es unmittelbar mit der Sprache selbst zu thun; das Object der Sprachwissenschaft ist also ein concretes, reelles, nämlich die bestimmten, gegebenen Sprachen" (Schleicher 1860:119). "La langue n'est pas moins que la parole un objet de natur concrète, et c'est un grand avantage pour l'étude. Les signes linguistiques, pour être essentiellement psychiques, ne sont pas des abstractions; les associations ratifiées par le consentement collectif, et dont l'ensemble constitue la langue, sont des réalités qui ont leur siège dans le cerveau" (Saussure 1916:32;1959:15). We will discuss later the issue of the psychological reality of language as a system of signs assumed here by Saussure.

4. ANALYSIS: THE DOMAIN OF PEOPLE

1. This is in contrast to the Stoic theory of sensation involving pneuma passing from the principle part of the psyche to the senses (Diogenes Laertius VII 52), their theory that the seat of rational speech is in the heart (Diogenes Laertius VII 159), and their theory that the world is a living being, rational, animate, and intelligent, endowed with sensation and a psyche (Diogenes Laertius VII 142–3). All of these have been discarded.

5. IMPLICATIONS

1. The plethora of types of grammar differing in the assumptions they make is not a modern development. Michael (1970) found 259 grammars of English written or printed in England between 1586 and 1800. They represent 56 different systems in terms just of what parts of speech they recognize.

2. The term *human linguistics* has been used at least since 1971. It is a generic term that denotes any linguistics that would study people, individually and collectively, rather than assumed objects of language, and that would study them directly from the point of view of how they communicate rather than through language and grammar, thus eliminating unsupported assumptions and introducing instead theories that can be tested against reality and that can then be judged on their merit as in the physical and biological sciences. Other uses of the term are to be discouraged.

6. A SCIENTIFIC FOUNDATION FOR LINGUISTICS

1. The first attempt at articulating a goal for linguistics along the present lines was reported in Yngve (1969). An early effort to work out properties in a state theory was reported in Yngve (1970), which also opted explicitly for science. By 1973 the goal of linguistics had been restated without language (Yngve 1975b,c,d), and the several types of linguistic properties had been delineated. Some recent reports are Yngve (1983, 1984, 1985, in press). The human linguistics effort began as an attempt to improve the linguistic foundation for the depth hypothesis (Yngve 1960) in a way that would preserve its insights and its ability to explain historical change (Yngve 1975a) without accepting the problems inherent in the grammatical tradition.

7. LAWS OF COMMUNICATIVE BEHAVIOR

1. Human linguistics is treated at the next level of detail in a work that is in preparation.

2. Characterizations of individuals or linkages to any degree of detail are complex enough that computer testing becomes essential for scientific progress. A computer simulator program has been developed that accepts human linguistics models expressed in the notation of the theory and runs them in order to test and debug them. This also provides a scientifically justified notation that can be used in computational linguistics and artificial intelligence.

8. THE LINGUISTIC STRUCTURE OF PROPERTIES OF PEOPLE

1. Additional notations and detailed justification are to be found in the larger work being prepared for publication.

10. TESTS OF THEORY AGAINST OBSERVATION

1. Chomsky defended this assumption by adding, "This seems to me to have been the position of the founders of modern general linguistics, and no cogent reason for modifying it has been offered." In the first place, the force of tradition is not sufficient justification for a special assumption. In the second place, special assumptions do not come for free in science. The burden of providing cogent reasons falls on those who would propose, accept, or retain them, not on those who would doubt them.

2. For a study of coherence in discourse comparing schizophrenic and normal speakers using a human-linguistics approach, see Lanin-Kettering (1983). For a study of the topic of conversation using an early version of human linguistics see Vance (1974).

3. This means, of course, that everything would be moved over that belongs in a linguistics focused on achieving a scientific understanding of how people communicate. Such a linguistics would not presume to claim areas outside of its domain. The precise location of the boundaries between scientific linguistics and other concerns such as ethics, aesthetics, and the theory of knowledge, which do have some communicative content, can probably not be estimated until scientific linguistics has been more fully developed. The issue of whether such other areas can be brought completely within the domain of science is not a question internal to linguistics.

REFERENCES

Aarsleff, Hans. 1967. *The study of language in England, 1780–1860*. Princeton: Princeton University Press.

Arnim, Hans F. A. von, ed. 1903. *Stoicorum veterum fragmenta*. 4 vols. Leipzig: B. G. Teubner.

Austin, John L. 1962. *How to do things with words*. Cambridge, Mass.: Harvard University Press. [New York: Oxford University Press. 1965.]

Barwick, Karl. 1922. *Remmius Palaemon und die römische Ars grammatica*. Leipzig: Dieterich'sche Verlagsbuchhandlung.

―――. 1925. *Flavii Sosipatri Charisii Artis grammaticae*. Leipzig: B. G. Teubner. [2d ed. 1964.]

Bickerton, Derek. 1973. The nature of a creole continuum. *Language* 49.640–69.

Binnick, Robert I. 1981. Review of *Modern linguistics*, by Neil Smith and Deirdre Wilson. *Language* 57.182–83.

Bloomfield, Leonard. 1926. A set of postulates for the science of language. *Language* 2.153–64.

―――. 1933. *Language*. New York: Holt. [Reprint. Chicago: University of Chicago Press. 1984.]

Botha, Rudolf P. 1971. *Methodological aspects of transformational generative phonology*. Janua Linguarum Series Minor, 112. The Hague: Mouton.

―――. 1973. *The justification of linguistic hypotheses: a study of nondemonstrative inference in transformational grammar*. Janua Linguarum Series Maior, 84. The Hague: Mouton.

Carnap, Rudolf. 1942. *Introduction to semantics*. Studies in Semantics, 1. Cambridge, Mass.: Harvard University Press.

Chomsky, Noam. 1965. *Aspects of the theory of syntax*. Cambridge, Mass.: MIT Press.

―――. 1970. Deep structure, surface structure, and semantic interpretation. In *Studies in general and oriental linguistics presented to Shirô Hattori on the occasion of his sixtieth birthday*, ed. Roman Jakobson and Shigeo Kawamoto, 52–91. Tokyo: TEC Company Ltd.

Coseriu, Eugenio. 1969. *Die Geschichte der Sprachphilosophie von der Antike bis zur Gegenwart: Eine Übersicht*. Vol. 1, *Von der Antike bis Leibniz*. Tübingen: Romanisches Seminar der Universität Tübingen.

Derwing, Bruce L. 1973. *Transformational grammar as a theory of language acquisition*. Cambridge: Cambridge University Press.

Dingwall, William Orr. 1971. *A survey of linguistic science*. College Park, Md: University of Maryland Linguistics Program. [2d ed. Stamford, Conn.: Greylock Publishers. 1978.]

Drake, Stillman. 1976. *Galileo against the philosophers*. Los Angeles: Zeitlin & Ver Brugge.

Egli, Urs. 1967. *Zur stoischen Dialektik*. Basel: Sandoz.

Engler, Rudolf, ed. 1967. *Ferdinand de Saussure: Cours de linguistique générale, édition critique*. Wiesbaden. Otto Harrassowitz.

Fick, August. 1871. *Vergleichendes Wörterbuch der indogermanischen Sprachen*. 2d. rev. ed. Göttingen: Vandenhoeck & Ruprecht's Verlag.

Foote, Kenneth E. 1983. *Color in public spaces: Toward a communication-based theory of the urban built environment*. The University of Chicago Department of Geography Research Paper No. 205. Chicago.

Gardiner, Alan H. 1932. *The theory of speech and language*. Oxford: Clarendon Press.

Gilliéron, Jules, and Mario Roques. 1912. *Études de géographie linguistique d'après l'Atlas linguistique de la France*. Paris: Librairie Honoré Champion, Éditeur.

Goffman, Erving. 1963. *Behavior in public places*. New York: The Free Press.

Gross, Maurice. 1979. On the failure of generative grammar. *Language* 55.859–85.

Gumperz, John J. 1962. Types of linguistic communities. *Anthropological Linguistics* 4(1).28–40.

Hall, Robert A., Jr. 1962. The life cycle of pidgin languages. *Lingua* 11.151–56.

Hicks, R. D., ed. 1925. *Diogenes Laertius: Lives of eminent philosophers*. 2 vols. London: William Heinemann. [Reprint. Cambridge, Mass.: Harvard University Press, 1980.]

Holden, Constance. 1985. An omnifarious data bank for biology? *Science* 228.1412.

Hülser, Karlheinz, ed. 1979. *Rudolf T. Schmidt: Die Grammatik der Stoiker*. Braunschweig and Wiesbaden: Friedr. Vieweg & Sohn.

Hutchinson, Larry G. 1974. Grammar as theory. In *Explaining linguistic phenomena*, ed. David Cohen, 43–73. New York: Wiley.

Hymes, Dell. 1962. The ethnography of speaking. In *Anthropology and human behavior*, ed. Thomas Gladwin and Wm. C. Sturtevant, 13–53. Washington, D.C.: Anthropological Society of Washington.

———. 1974. *Foundations in sociolinguistics: An ethnographic approach*. Philadelphia: University of Pennsylvania Press.

Jakobson, Roman. 1965. Quest for the essence of language. *Diogenes* 51.21–37.

Keil, Heinrich, ed. 1864. *Gramatici Latini*. Vol. 4. Leipzig: B. G. Teubner.

Kent, Roland G., ed. 1938. *Varro: On the Latin language*. 2 vols. Cambridge, Mass.: Harvard University Press. [Reprint. 1967.]

Labov, William. 1963. The social motivation of a sound change. *Word* 19.273–309.

Lamb, Sydney M. 1966. *Outline of stratificational grammar*. Washington, D.C.: Georgetown University Press.

Lanin-Kettering, Ilene. 1983. Toward a communicative model of discourse cohesion. Ph.D. diss., The University of Chicago.

Lehmann, Winfred P. 1967. See Osthoff and Brugmann 1878.

Lewin, Roger. 1985. Slime molds on wings. *Science* 228:1416.

Linsky, Leonard. 1967. *Referring*. London: Routledge & Kegan Paul. [Reprint. 1969.]

Malinowski, Bronislaw. 1937. The dilemma of contemporary linguistics. *Nature* 140.172–73.

Mates, Benson. 1953. *Stoic logic*. University of California Publications in Philosophy 26. Berkeley and Los Angeles: University of California Press.

Michael, Ian. 1970. *English grammatical categories and the tradition to 1800*. London: Cambridge University Press.

Morris, Charles W. 1938. Foundations of the theory of signs. In *Foundations of the unity of science*. Vol. 1, no. 2, of *International encyclopedia of unified science*, ed. Otto Neurath. Chicago: University of Chicago Press.

Naro, Anthony J. 1978. A study of the origins of pidginization. *Language* 54.314–47.

———. 1980. Review of *Linguistic variation: Models and methods*, ed. David Sankoff. *Language* 56.158–70.

Osthoff, Hermann and Karl Brugman 1878. *Morphologische Untersuchungen auf dem*

Gebiete der indogermanischen Sprachen. Part 1. Leipzig: S. Hirzel. [Foreword translated in *A reader in nineteenth-century historical Indo-European linguistics*, ed. Winfred P. Lehmann, 198–209. Bloomington: Indiana University Press, 1967.]

Parret, Herman. 1974. *Discussing language*. Janua Linguarum Series Maior, 93. The Hague: Mouton.

Paul, Hermann. 1889. *Principles of the history of language*. Trans. H. A. Strong. New York: Macmillan.

Pfeiffer, Rudolf. 1968. *History of classical scholarship from the beginnings to the end of the Hellenistic age*. Oxford: Clarendon Press.

Pike, Kenneth L. 1967. *Language in relation to a unified theory of the structure of human behavior*. Janua Linguarum Series Maior, 24. 2d. rev. ed. The Hague and Paris: Mouton.

Pinborg, Jan. 1975. Classical antiquity: Greece. *Current trends in linguistics* 13.69–126.

Rask, Rasmus. 1830. En Forelæsning over Sprogets Filosofi. MS. written in 1830. [Published in his *Ausgewählte Abhandlungen*, ed. Louis Hjelmslev, 2.375–78. Copenhagen: Levin & Munksgaard, 1932–33.]

Ringen, Jon D. 1975. Linguistic facts: a study of the empirical scientific status of transformational generative grammars. In *Testing linguistic hypotheses*, ed. David Cohen and Jessica R. Wirth, 1–41. New York: Wiley.

Robins, R. H. 1951. *Ancient & mediaeval grammatical theory in Europe with particular reference to modern linguistic doctrine*. London: G. Bell & Sons Ltd.

———. 1958. Dionysius Thrax and the western grammatical tradition. *Transactions of the Philological Society* 1957.67–106.

Robinson, Ian. 1975. *The new grammarians' funeral: a critique of Noam Chomsky's linguistics*. Cambridge: Cambridge University Press.

Sandys, John Edwin. 1915. *A short history of classical scholarship from the sixth century B.C. to the present day*. Cambridge: Cambridge University Press.

Sapir, Edward. 1921. *Language: An introduction to the study of speech*. New York: Harcourt, Brace.

———. 1929. The status of linguistics as a science. *Language* 5.207–14.

Saussure, Ferdinand de. 1916. *Cours de linguistique générale publié par Charles Bally et Albert Sechehaye avec la collaboration de Albert Riedlinger*. Lausanne and Paris: Payot. [*Course in general linguistics*, trans. Wade Baskin. New York: McGraw-Hill, 1959.]

Schleicher, August. 1850. *Die Sprachen Europas in systematischer Uebersicht*. Linguistische Untersuchungen, 2. Bonn: H. B. König.

———. 1859. *Zur Morphologie der Sprache*. Mémoires de l'académie impériale des sciences de St.-Pétersbourgh. 7th series, vol. 1, no. 7. [Often cataloged as Akademiia nauk, Petrograd. Mémoires. 1859.]

———. 1860. *Die deutsche Sprache*. Stuttgart: Verlag der J. G. Cotta'schen Buchhandlung. [5th ed. 1888.]

———. 1865. *Über die Bedeutung der Sprache für die Naturgeschichte des Menschen*. Weimar: Hermann Böhlau.

Schmidt, Johannes. 1872. *Die Verwantschaftsverhältnisse der indogermanischen Sprachen*. Weimar: Hermann Böhlau.

Sebeok, Thomas A. 1974. Semiotics. A survey of the state of the art. *Current trends in linguistics* 12.211–64.

Silverstein, Michael. 1972. Chinook Jargon: Language contact and the problem of multi-level generative systems. *Language* 48:378–406, 596–625.

Thomsen, Vilhelm. 1889. Rasmus Kristian Rask (1787–1887). *Beiträge zur Kunde der indogermanischen Sprachen herausgegeben von Dr. Adalbert Bezzenberger* 14.317–30.

Twaddell, W. Freeman. 1935. *On defining the phoneme*. Language Monograph 16.

Vance, Stuart-Morgan. 1974. Conversational alternation and the topic of conversation. Ph.D. diss., The University of Chicago.

Watson, John Selby, ed. and trans. 1856. *Quintilian's Institutes of oratory: or, education of an orator*. Vol. 1. London: Henry G. Bohn.

Weinreich, Uriel; William Labov; and Marvin I. Herzog. 1968. Empirical foundations for a theory of language change. In *Directions for historical linguistics*, ed. W. P. Lehmann and Yakov Malkiel, 98–195. Austin: University of Texas Press.

Whitney, William Dwight. 1867. *Language and the study of language*. New York: Charles Scribner's Sons. [5th ed. 1891.]

Wilks, Yorick Alexander. 1972. *Grammar, meaning and the machine analysis of language*. London: Routledge & Kegan Paul.

Yngve, Victor H. 1960. A model and an hypothesis for language structure. *Proceedings of the American Philosophical Society* 104:444–66.

———. 1969. On achieving agreement in linguistics. In *Papers from the fifth regional meeting of the Chicago Linguistic Society*, ed. R. I. Binnick et al., 455–62. Chicago: Department of Linguistics, The University of Chicago.

———. 1970. On getting a word in edgewise. In *Papers from the sixth regional meeting, Chicago Linguistic Society*, ed. M. A. Campbell et al., 567–78. Chicago: Chicago Linguistic Society.

———. 1975a. Depth and the historical change of the English genitive. *Journal of English Linguistics* 9.47–57.

———. 1975b. The dilemma of contemporary linguistics. In *The first LACUS forum 1974*, ed. Adam Makkai and Valerie Becker Makkai, 1–16. Columbia, South Carolina: Hornbeam Press.

———. 1975c. Human linguistics and face-to-face interaction. In *Organization of behavior in face-to-face interaction*, ed. Adam Kendon et al. World Anthropology, gen. ed. Sol Tax. The Hague: Mouton. Also in *Socialization and communication in primary groups*, ed. Thomas R. Williams. World Anthropology, gen. ed. Sol Tax. The Hague: Mouton.

———. 1975d. Toward a human linguistics. In *Papers from the Parasession on Functionalism*, ed. R. E. Grossman et al., 540–55. Chicago: Chicago Linguistic Society.

———. 1981. The struggle for a theory of Native Speaker. In *A Festschrift for Native Speaker*, ed. Florian Coulmas, 29–49. Janua Linguarum Series Maior, 97. The Hague: Mouton.

———. 1983. Bloomfield's fundamental assumption of linguistics. In *The ninth LACUS forum 1982*, ed. John Morreall, 137–45. Columbia, South Carolina: Hornbeam Press.

———. 1984. The law of componential partitioning. In *The tenth LACUS forum 1983*, ed. Alan Manning et al., 108–16. Columbia, South Carolina: Hornbeam Press.

———. 1985. Concepts of system in science and in linguistics. In *The eleventh LACUS forum 1984*, ed. Robert A. Hall, Jr., 63–70. Columbia, South Carolina: Hornbeam Press.

———. in press. The pragmatic aspects of human linguistics. In *The twelfth LACUS forum 1985*.

INDEX AND GUIDE

Headings in *italic* type constitute a guide to human linguistics terms and concepts introduced and other related technical terms used. Page numbers in *italics* type indicate definitions or main explanations.